WHOSE DEATH
IS IT ANYWAY?

WHOSE DEATH IS IT ANYWAY?

Euthanasia and the Right to Die

John Scally

First published in Ireland in 1995 by
Basement Press
an imprint of Attic Press Ltd
29 Upper Mount Street
Dublin 2

A catalogue record for this title is available from the British Library

ISBN 185594 141 4

Origination: Verbatim Typesetting and Design
Printing: The Guernsey Press Co. Ltd

This book is published with the assistance of The Arts Council/An Chomhairle Ealaíon, Ireland.

Dedication

To my aunt Lizzie in gratitude for her many
kindnesses.

Acknowledgments

I would like to express my thanks to my former teacher Raphael Gallagher who nurtured my interest in medical ethics initially. I am also grateful to Maurice Reidy for his encouragement and many kindnesses to me in recent years.

I also wish to express my gratitude to Werner Jeanrond who played a pivotal role in my academic development, and also to the Theology Department in Trinity College, particularly Professor Séan Freyne for his encouragement.. My thanks also to Tom O'Dowd, of the Community Health Department, Trinity College, for his interest in my work in this area and his practical assistance.

I am grateful to Róisín Conroy for inviting me to publish with Basement Press and to Maeve Kneafsey for her interest. Very special thanks to Ríona MacNamara, who suggested this book initially, for her support and encouragement.

Contents

Introduction

The phone rings three times.

'Hello, Dr Brown speaking. (Slight pause.) Thank you, nurse, please send him into my office.'

Knock on the door.

'Come on in, Mr Williams.'

'Good morning, doctor, thank you for seeing me. I know you have a busy schedule.'

'It's no trouble, Mr Williams. Please take a seat. Now what can I do for you?'

'It's about my mother.'

'Ah yes, I thought it might be.'

'You probably hadn't realised this but it's exactly a year today you told me she had terminal cancer.'

'I really had no idea. Gosh, is it that long?'

'I tried to put on a brave face for her sake, and she tried to cope with it as best she could.'

'It's a tragic case, but I'm afraid I see this kind of thing all too often.'

'I'm sure you do. The reason for my visit is to ask you to do something for my mother.'

'I'll be happy to do all I can.'

'Wait until you hear what I propose first. As you know, over the last three months my mother's condition has deteriorated alarmingly. She has wasted away to just a former shell of her old self. She hasn't been lucid for six weeks. She is enduring horrific pain. She hasn't spoken for six weeks. The only sounds she makes are small screams of pain. She hasn't the energy to do anything else. She hasn't recognised me for the last two months. She has become a human vegetable. She isn't living, she is existing, and each day brings nothing but still more pain and anguish. In the name of mercy and compassion I want her to die with a shred of dignity before she goes through much more agony, and I need your help.'

'Let me intervene at this point. I am truly sorry for what your mother is going through and I fully understand your motivation, but I cannot be party to euthanasia. I took an oath to protect life, not to take it.'

'Yes, but what kind of life? Surely you also took an oath to ensure some quality of life? Surely preserving life cannot be an end in itself. Your oath cannot be a weapon of cruelty and it is nothing but cruelty to keep old people, who have lost the will to live, in agony in a hospital bed. My mother has had a long and good life. All I want is for her to die with a little bit of dignity. She has suffered far too much as it is.'

'I can't disagree with you on that point, but equally I cannot break the law which forbids me from killing people.'

'Which is more important to you, to keep the law or to be humane? It cannot be humane to let my mother's anguished existence go any longer. I'm not asking you to kill my mother. I've got some chemicals here in a syringe in my bag – don't ask me where or how I got them – which will put my mother into a blissful sleep from which she will never wake up. All I am asking is for you to turn a blind eye while I inject her.'

Such have been the advances of technological advancement that Dr Brown's and Mr Williams's predicament is not unusual. Reporting the problem is one thing – finding answers is much more difficult. It is the task of this book to investigate the legal, medical, social, political and ethical issues raised by euthanasia.

THERE ARE MORE QUESTIONS THAN ANSWERS

Robert Browning once wrote:

> Grow old along with me
> the best is yet to be
> the last of life for which the first was made.

This sentiment has a very hollow ring to it at the end of the twentieth century, because of advances of medical technology. Indeed, Charles Dickens's comment 'It was the best of times. It was the worst of times' may be much more appropriate. Modern medicine can call upon an amazing arsenal of weapons to keep a person alive almost indefinitely. This brings its own problems.

Since birth and death define the limits of human existence, they accordingly occupy a prominent position in any ethical theory. As a norm, life is deemed to have a high value, and death conversely is considered to have a negative value. Advances in medicine have created a situation where, in many cases, health-care professionals can postpone death for lengthy periods. Such power raises major ethical issues, particularly in relation to five questions:

- Is life always preferable to death?
- If not, by what criteria is life considered to be intolerable?

- Are there some circumstances in which the value of a particular human life can be overridden?
- If so, what ethical principles should be referred to in such situations?
- In conflict situations, how are doctors to reconcile their commitment to relieve suffering with their commitment to prolong life?

These problems are further complicated when life can be maintained for a significant period if the patient accepts dependence on a drug, a procedure, or a machine. In such circumstances death may be postponed, but the quality of life may be greatly impaired. Particular difficulties arise in paediatrics and in the area of consent, particularly when the guardians request withdrawal of treatment contrary to medical advice.

A RIGHT TO DIE?

To talk of death is difficult and often unpleasant. To listen may be even more problematic. 'I wouldn't want to live like that' is a sentiment that unleashes a cascade of emotions and prompts denial, tension and flight. Historically, there has always been a strong social taboo, reflected in virtually all ethical theories, against causing death. In recent years, though, people have begun to demand what they want or need as matter of rights, for example the right to education, employment, a clean environment, a right to privacy. The newest addition to this list of rights is said to be the right to die.

The right to die is asserted against the background of dramatically altered circumstances and fears about treatment at the end of life. Because of the advances in medical care that we have already discussed, many who would previously be dead are alive only because of sustained medical intervention. In many cases, death is preceded by some explicit decision about terminating or not beginning treatment. Increasingly, death is not simply medically managed, but its timing is also subject to deliberate choice. It is for this reason that euthanasia has surfaced as a prominent topic of debate.

'Euthanasia' is a composite term derived from two Greek words – *eu*, meaning 'well', and *thantos*, meaning 'death' – and means 'good death' or 'painless, happy death'. A dictionary definition of euthanasia is the 'painless inducement of a quick death'. However, this definition is seriously flawed: I could sneak up behind my local revenue commissioner and silently inject him with a painless and fast-acting drug, causing him to have a quick and painless death, but this would be murder, not euthanasia. The simplicity of the dictionary definition is overly simplistic. A more adequate definition would include considerations of suffering or disease, and the reasons an administering agent has for causing the death of another human being.

In recent years, two major court cases in the United Kingdom, those of Dr Nigel Cox and Mr Tony Bland, generated huge media and public interest and focused attention on the questions of euthanasia, assisted suicide and the ethical complexities which these issues entail. In the first case, Dr Cox was prosecuted for administering a lethal injection to a patient who was dying in unbearable pain. In the Tony Bland case, the courts were asked by his parents to authorise the withdrawal of all procedures, including feeding, from their son, who was in a persistent vegetative state arising from horrific injuries sustained in the 1989 Hillsborough football disaster.

A distinction is sometimes made between 'active

euthanasia', i.e. administering a lethal drug, and 'passive euthanasia', i.e. the non-administration of life-saving drugs or the withdrawal of life-support systems. However, in popular usage the term 'euthanasia' has also come to be associated with an interventionist act of 'mercy killing'. Euthanasia raises a number of difficult legal and ethical issues. Many people would say that a doctor who gives a terminally ill patient a lethal drug for the purpose of terminating that patient's life is acting outside the limits of ethically acceptable behaviour, but what of a doctor who, at the request of a patient's family, turns off a respirator which is keeping a comatose patient alive? What of a doctor who removes intravenous tubes providing a terminally ill patient with hydration and nourishment? How are we to decide when a patient is dead, for example in a case of the patient whose brain has been destroyed but whose heart and lungs are still functioning?

At the core of the ethical controversy lies two fundamental questions. How are we to decide when a person is dead? How are we to decide which treatment is or is not appropriate for a terminally ill patient?

President John F. Kennedy, shortly after his election, claimed that the key issue of the modern times is the management of industrial society – a problem of ways and means, not of ideology:

'The fact of the matter is that most of the problems, or at least many of them, that we now face are technical problems, are administrative problems [necessitating] ... very sophisticated judgements which do not lend themselves to the great sort of "passionate movements" which have stirred this country so often in the past.'

His analysis has proven to be seriously defective, in so far as philosophical questions continue to be crucially important in finding answers to the value-related issues which have emerged with technological progress. As we shall see, euthanasia raises a plethora of such value-related questions. One such question is: how are we to define death? It is to this question I now turn.

One

The Moment of Death

Up until recent times, death was defined in medical terms as the complete and persistent cessation of respiration and circulation, but technological developments now facilitate the artificial maintenance of circulation and respiration even after the brain has been destroyed. It is easy to see the attraction of the traditional criteria, since their absence gave a presumption of death – so why move away from them? The reason is that life is no longer seen as a collection of processes, but as an coordinated system where the nervous system in the brain plays a central coordinating role, so that without some brain functioning the whole system of life cannot be sustained. On a purely practical level, new criteria are needed because of advances in life-support machines which allow us to maintain blood circulation artificially and to maintain breathing well beyond the point where, previously, death would have occurred.

From the ethical viewpoint the question is: what is essential to the nature of a person, the loss of which would warrant calling someone dead? The new criteria for death that eventually emerged was that of 'brain death'. In 1968 an *ad hoc* committee of the Harvard Medical School formulated a set of criteria for 'irreversible coma'. Their report took into account the improvements in resuscitation and life-support machines which meant that 'life' could be sustained in a previously inconceivable way, and, further, the fact that obsolete definitions of death can lead to controversy around subjects such as organ transplants. Their full definition is 'irreversible coma in the sense that the comatose individual has no discernible central nervous system activity'. This is to be determined by:

- total unawareness and complete unresponsiveness to recognised tests and stimuli;
- the establishment of the total absence of spontaneous breathing;
- the absence of elicitable responses;
- the above three conditions to be confirmed, where possible, by EEG and ECG tests. It is important to stress the word 'irreversible' because the possibility of certain drug intoxication and abnormally low body temperatures could produce temporary effects which would preclude a doctor from declaring that brain death was permanent.

The judgement as to whether death has occurred or not is primarily a medical one, not an ethical one, as acknowledged by Pope Pius XII in his address 'The Prolongation of Life' in 1958.

Brain death has replaced the respiration/ circulation criteria, because a working brain is an essential prerequisite for all those qualities that we equate with being human. This is not to imply that one is required to possess all of these abilities, otherwise the severely mentally disabled, for example, would not be considered persons. The criteria for determining whether a patient is dead must not be confused with criteria for determining when certain kinds of treatment (for example the use of respirators) may be withheld or stopped.

We must distinguish at this point between the concept of 'the death of the organism as a whole', i.e. when the brain has died, and the 'death of the whole organism', i.e. the death of all the cells of an organism. It is this distinction which allows us to say that a person is dead when their brain is dead, even though other organs may be functioning because of artificial means.

Articulating a definition is essentially a conceptual problem rather than an ethical one. However, many ethical decisions rest on it. When there is no brain function associated with such existence, it is difficult to claim that the patient is alive, even though the heart continues its assisted beating. Moreover, there is a huge expense attached to these procedures and the ancillary treatment. Legal arrangements, for example when to execute the patient's will, are confused because the ambiguous state of these patients leaves such affairs in a legal limbo. If such life-support systems were to be turned off, the patient's undamaged organs could be lifesavers if used for transplants.

The Harvard definition assumes without argument that death is equated with brain death, which in turn is equated with the clinical condition of irreversible coma. Is this a legitimate position? A definition of death is not framed in isolation but against the broader canvas of our understanding of personal life.

REST IN PEACE

There have been a number of different efforts to improve the Harvard definition. One of America's foremost ethicists, Daniel Callahan, has attempted to define natural death as when:

1. one's life work has been accomplished;
2. one's ethical obligation's to those for whom one has responsibilities have been discharged;
3. one's death will not seem to others an offence to sense or sensibility, or will not tempt others to despair and rage at human existence;
4. one's process of dying is not marked by unbearable and degrading pain.

The problem with this approach is that all four points are ambiguous.

In an article entitled 'Death: Process or Event?' (1971), Robert Morison argued that death cannot properly be understood as an event, but is more correctly seen as a process that begins with birth. In this perspective life and death are a continuum, and therefore death cannot occur at a specific moment. This is little short of nonsense, because it makes living synonymous with dying. Taken to its limits, one could argue that murder could be considered a far-sighted form of euthanasia, a gift to the dying of an early exit from the miseries of old age. Such a position confuses ageing with dying, and the process of death with death itself. More positively, it does remind us of the need to consider the relationship between the meaning of death and the criteria used to determine the time of the event of death.

Economists propose different ways to determine the value of life, for example discounted future earnings.

Such approaches bring problems of their own – notably the effect of tending to give priority to young adult white males. The American ethicist Paul Ramsey offers a 'primitive' example which may be helpful since it takes the issue away from medical technology and into the realms of common sense. A boy-scout leader led a group of scouts into a remote area by the sea. Against express orders, one of the scouts dived off the cliffs into the sea for a swim. Tragically, the youngster crashed his head off a rock, shattering his brain. No medical help was available. The scout leader applied mouth-to-mouth resuscitation and chest artificial respiration for some time. Eventually he stopped and declared the boy dead. It would have made no sense for him to tell the family that he made his determination on the basis of the nature of his head injury and while the boy's heart was still spontaneously beating. The attempts to respirate him were abandoned when it was clear that he was already dead. Ramsey deserves credit for trying to introduce common sense into the debate, but his example resolves few of the difficult questions about defining death.

The Danish Council of Ethics (DCE) argues that contemporary medical criteria for brain death should not be accepted as criteria for death, though they should be accepted as criteria for the irreversible onset of the death process. They argue that the criterion for death should still be the cessation of cardiac activity, basing its conclusion on the concept of death in everyday experience and its ethical implications. The DCE are prompted by the wish that all medical criteria for death should correspond to lay people's notion of death. This assumes, with undue haste, that medical criteria for brain death do not correspond to lay people's concept of death. The DCE appear to suggest that 'ordinary people' view death as being the cessation of existence of a person, and that the ethical concern of people for people is not adequately expressed in the scientific concept of death as the death of the brain. They argue that 'in science death is not regarded as a person's death but rather as the cessation of the life functions of a biological organism'. The DCE are correct to distinguish between death of biological organisms and death of persons. However, its distinction between the ordinary concept of death and scientific death is unnecessary, since the World Medical Association's declaration of Sydney on death explicitly affirms that clinical interest lies 'in the fate of a person'. The DCE are also correct to point out that one of the problems with using the brain-death definition is that it is difficult for lay people to detect and understand when this has taken place. While the traditional criteria of the absence of respiration and circulation are easily established, it has to be acknowledged that essential to being a person is the capacity, or potential capacity, for consciousness. When a person has permanently lost the capacity for consciousness, the person is dead.

A number of efforts have been made to try to develop objective standards for assessment of the individual patient's condition – though 'objective' is a problematic word. Whose objectivity? Who decides who decides? One possible criteria developed in family medicine was 'functional status', that is a measure of a patient's overall physical, emotional and social wellbeing. It was defined in 1992 by Scholten and Van Weel as 'the level of functioning of a certain patient and at a certain moment or in a given period of time'. A patient's functional status is assessed by the use of a core set of functional aspects: physical fitness, feelings, daily and social activities, change in health and overall health.

As It Was in The Beginning

The importance of determining when the dying process begins may also be relevant at the beginning of life. For example, in the USA in the 1960s Bernard Bard confessed that when he became the father of a Down's Syndrome son, he wished the boy would die. He explicitly requested that the doctors should do nothing to extend his son's life artificially, and he was assured that the institution to which he committed his son contained no supplies of oxygen, nor did it provide inoculation against childhood disease. Eventually the young boy died of heart failure and jaundice. Is this a case of 'letting die' or 'putting to death'? In ethical terms there is very little difference between this kind of case and the cases of Down's Syndrome children born with digestive obstructions which parents refuse to allow doctors to operate on, thus condemning these children to the slow death of starvation. Such actions do not constitute 'cooperating with the dying process'.

Legal cases highlight the need for a more refined reflection about the moment of death. One such case was that of Mr Bruce Tucker, who was used as a heart donor after he had suffered massive brain damage in an accident. His brother took a case against the doctors who performed the transplant, contending that Mr Tucker was alive when the heart was taken, since machines were maintaining respiration and blood flow.

Organ transplantations from brain-dead patients are

now commonplace in many developed countries, but they still remain a taboo in Japan because of the lack of a national consensus. This is despite the report of a governmental commission in January 1992 on the issue of brain death and organ transplantation, which allowed organ transplantations from brain-dead patients. However, no transplantations had been done up to a study in September 1993, and the police authorities are still adopting the cardio-pulmonary criteria of death in coroner's inquests. Although more than half of respondents to public opinion polls approved organ transplantation from brain-dead patients, many ardent opponents remain. The reluctance of Japanese people to accepting brain death as the death of a person can be attributed to the following:

1. *A distrust of practitioners.* The first heart transplantation in Japan was performed in 1968 by a Professor Wada. However, strong doubts emerged regarding the diagnosis of brain death of the donor and the surgical indication for the operation of the recipient. Consequently Professor Wada was accused of murder. Since that incident, popular mistrust in the physicians who intend to do organ transplantations has grown, and surgeons have kept away from doing transplantation from brain-dead patients because of the fear of being sued.
2. *Distinctions between relatives and strangers.* Many parents have donated kidneys or parts of the liver to their children. However, few people have registered in the donor-card system which is intended to facilitate organ transplantations to anonymous non-relatives.
3. *Priority of families to individuals.* Under the principle of

informed consent the decision of the individual, has priority over all other agents. The situation in Japan is that individuals are subjects to the decision of their families, even when they have decided to donate their organs.

4. *Attachment to the remains.* For example, when relatives are lost in aeroplane accidents, Japanese people are known to go to the tops of mountains to seek for even a tiny part of the remains. Their belief is that the soul resides in every part of the remains, so the removal of organs prior to funeral is repugnant to the traditional sensitivities of the Japanese people.

5. *Feeling of reluctance based on the common sense.* They see a brain-dead person and find it difficult to believe that this warm, pulsating body is really dead. It goes against their ordinary idea of death.

6. *A gradual acceptance of the death on the part of relatives.* The diagnosis of death does not necessarily mean the death of the patient to the relatives. When death is diagnosed by the doctor, there begins a long series of rituals that help people to realise gradually that the deceased is gone forever. Accordingly, it goes against their culture to identify the diagnosis of brain death with the death of the person. The understanding of when death occurs is also of pivotal importance in decisions about the treatment of terminally ill patients.

A REDUNDANT CONCEPT

Traditionally ethicists have distinguished between 'ordinary means' and 'extraordinary means' in making decisions about the treatment of terminally ill patients. The distinction between the two has been clearly defined by Paul Ramsey:

Ordinary means of preserving life are all medicines, treatments, and operations, which offer a reasonable hope of benefit for the patient and which can be obtained and used without excessive expense, pain, and other inconveniences. Extraordinary means of preserving life are all those medicines, treatments, and operations which cannot be obtained without excessive expense, pain, or other inconvenience, or which, if used, would not offer a reasonable hope of benefit.

The problem with this distinction is twofold. Firstly, such is the pace of technological advancement that what is extraordinary today may well be ordinary tomorrow. Secondly, it lacks precision. How are we to decide what treatment 'would not offer a reasonable hope of benefit', particularly when there is a divergence of opinion between the relevant health-care professionals? Who decides?

The distinction between ordinary and extraordinary means was born in Roman Catholic theology in the sixteenth century by the Spanish theologian Dominic Banez, who claimed that while it was reasonable to require people to conserve their lives by ordinary means such as ordinary nourishment, clothing and medicine, even at the cost of ordinary pain or suffering, people were not morally required to inflict on themselves extraordinary pain or anguish or undertakings that were disproportionate to their state in life.

The term 'extraordinary' is elastic, so that what might be considered 'extraordinary' in one set of circumstances might be ordinary in another. Using a respirator to treat a patient with respiratory disease is 'ordinary', whereas its use to sustain the life of a severely brain-damaged person in an irreversible coma would be considered 'extraordinary'. 'Ordinary' treatment refers to the 'normal' (clearly this too is an ambiguous term) care a doctor might be expected to provide. A failure to offer such care represents neglect, and, where there is a legal obligation to provide care, could be seen as the intentional infliction of harm.

The essence of the extraordinary/ordinary distinction is largely on the level of the doctor's intention. Withholding extraordinary care should be seen as a decision not to inflict painful treatment on a patient without a reasonable hope of success. On the other hand, withholding of ordinary care must be seen as neglect. It is not possible to say with any conviction what will be incurable in the future unless health care becomes stationary and sterile.

In deciding between ordinary and extraordinary means, reference is often made to the balance of benefits and burdens. However, this method is useless until what counts as a benefit or a burden can be determined, how much those benefits and burdens are to count, and whose benefits or burdens are to be counted. It is particularly important to clarify whose good is to be examined. Are such decisions meant to free the patient from the tyranny of an imperative to keep alive at all costs? Or are they designed to free society from the burden and expense of caring for a growing multitude of patients who require expensive care?

Another major problem with the ordinary/extraordinary distinction is the interpretation of the word 'hopeless'. An assessment of a patient's hopelessness must include such factors as the severity of their suffering, physical and psychological; their proximity to death; and an appropriate weighting of quality and quantity of life. A judgement about the quality of life ought not be determined by any one single quality, for example self-determination, but will encompass the variety, complexity and interplay of the qualities that we value. One possible criterion by which to assess when medical efforts ought to be made to try to preserve life, and when they ought to be suspended, is the potential for human relationships. Such a condition is an integral part of human life, and life without human relationships does not constitute human life at all.

Although the doctrine of ordinary/extraordinary means is poorly named, and it is more helpful to speak of 'proportionate' and 'disproportionate' means, it has a valuable insight to offer. In deciding on how much doctors should strive to keep their patients alive, it puts the emphasis on respect for the patient's own assessment of whether the struggle to stay alive would entail acceptable or excessive burdens, taking into account not just burdens on themselves but those on their families and others.

A HUMAN TRAGEDY

One of the incidents that brought these problems to light was the celebrated Karen Ann Quinlan case. She was a twenty-two-year-old woman who collapsed and ceased breathing for at least two fifteen-minute periods. When she was taken to hospital she gradually became deeply comatose over the following couple of days. As the weeks passed by, it emerged that she had suffered severe brain damage and was in a chronic vegetative state. Her father, a devout Catholic, consulted two priests and then requested the physician to withdraw her life-support mechanism. As the doctor did not feel free to make that decision on his own authority, Mr Quinlan applied to the court to be appointed her guardian, with the power to authorise discontinuance of all extraordinary medical treatment which he was informed was sustaining his daughter.

The Supreme Court of New Jersey, in a landmark decision given in 1976, found that a right of privacy was broad enough to encompass a patient's decision to refuse medical treatment under certain circumstances. It was not influenced by the ethical principles which were operative in the medical profession at the time, which required that life-support systems be maintained. In reaching its conclusion the Court was influenced by the brief submitted by the New Jersey Catholic Conference, which claimed that a decision to terminate those medical procedures which could be characterised as 'extraordinary means of treatment' did not involve euthanasia. However, the court case did not end the matter – once the support system was withdrawn, Karen began spontaneous respiration and continued to breathe naturally for a lengthy period. The Quinlan case highlights the inadequacy of using the 'extraordinary means' criteria as a reliable means of ethical reasoning in such cases. Withdrawing the 'extraordinary means' was clearly not a solution in this case. I wish to support a new understanding which has emerged in both legal and philosophical circles.

The Supreme Court of California, in the case of *Barber* v. *Superior Court of Los Angeles County,* halted a prosecution against surgeons charged with murder after they had terminated life-support measures given to a deeply comatose patient. In pointing out the difficulties of establishing precise guidelines, it suggested that the use of the terms 'ordinary' and 'extraordinary' measures was not helpful, and observed that a more rational approach was to determine whether the proposed treatment was 'proportionate' or 'disproportionate' in terms of the benefits to be gained versus the harm caused. This new terminology has also being employed in the *Declaration on Euthanasia* issued by the Vatican on 5 May 1980. Such an approach is much more helpful than the ambiguous concept of 'ordinary' and 'extraordinary'.

Another noteworthy feature of the Barber case was that it stipulated that the benefits and burdens of medical nutrition and hydration ought to be evaluated in the same manner as other mechanical devices, such as respirators, and that legally no distinction should be drawn between them. The importance of this provision was that it ensured that a decision taken to discontinue nutritional support in the case of a terminally ill incompetent patient would not attract any criminal liability.

CONCLUSION

This understanding highlights the fact that, while doctors do not have an obligation to prolong life beyond all reasonable expectations, it is important to be aware of the positive ethical values embodied in the practitioner's attempt to sustain life. The doctor's commitment to keep the patient's physiological organism, apart from the patient's other qualities, functioning is an affirmation of the doctor's duty to care for all patients equally, irrespective of their potential value to others. Perhaps terms such as 'brain death' or 'heart death' should be avoided, because what we are really searching for is the meaning of death of the person as a whole. Although it is cruel not to attempt to sustain life, it may be equally cruel to extend care unconditionally.

Two

The End Justifies the Means?

In the summer of 1989 a storm erupted in Germany when the Australian-based academic Peter Singer, author of *Practical Ethics* (1984), was invited to give a lecture titled 'Bioengineering, Ethics, and Mental Retardation', at a meeting in Marburg. Singer argues in favour of active euthanasia for severely disabled newborn infants if the parents request it. Shortly before the Marburg lecture where he planned to discuss the issue, it emerged that protest demonstrations had been planned both by organisations of disabled people and by opponents of biotechnology. These groups accused Singer of denying disabled people the right to life and, by questioning an absolute right to life, of having begun the slide along the same slippery slope that ended in the barbarism of Hitler. The organisers withdrew Singer's invitation and finally the lecture was cancelled. The cancellation spawned an explosive sequel – a major controversy about the limits and responsibilities of academic freedom. Does the right to free speech extend to the public propagation of murderous positions? Does academic freedom extend to the discussion of murderous positions? Philosophy classes and lectures were disrupted, and conferences had to be cancelled because of popular opposition as the battle lines were clearly drawn.

Opponents label Singer's position variously as 'deadly ethics' and 'new killing ethics', and Singer himself as 'a Nazi'. German critics in particular felt that they had a special duty to warn of the proverbial slippery slope. Their words of warning were taken very seriously by a German audience, even though they were not comparing the fanaticism of Hitler with those who support euthanasia from compassion. However, the fact that practically the entire German population stood idly by during the Nazi mass crimes is taken as a sufficient warning against any relativisation whatsoever of the sanctity of human life.

Until the Singer affair, active euthanasia of newborns, or other forms of non-voluntary euthanasia, was not discussed openly in Germany. There had been some support for the opinion that laws against voluntary euthanasia were irrational and inhumane. In 1980 the 'German Society of Humane Dying' was established to win a broader consensus for this insight. It was not until 1984 that the debate gained momentum in the wake of the extraordinarily dramatic self-accusations of Dr Julius Hackethal. He invited suits for active euthanasia in a number of cases, but was acquitted, as all that could be proved was that he had assisted in the suicide of terminal patients. Many people were afraid that public acceptance of voluntary euthanasia might have suffered a fatal blow at the hands of Hackethal's desire for publicity. Since 1985 opinion polls have shown that about two-thirds of Germans favour the legalisation of active voluntary euthanasia. In 1986 a number of esteemed lawyers and doctors published a carefully crafted 'Alternative Draft of a Law for Aid in Dying' that recommended against punishing doctors who fulfill their patients' final wishes for active euthanasia. The fifty-sixth Conference of German Lawyers and the German Physicians' Association rejected the draft by majority vote. After the Singer affair, discussion about active euthanasia in Germany is widespread.

ACTIVE OR PASSIVE?

A recurring problem in health care is the attempt to reconcile the belief in the sanctity of human life with considerations about quality of life when patients are terminally ill. In particular circumstances the medical decision may be that a patient's life is of such a low quality that it may not be worth living, and that no individual should be forced to continue living under such circumstances. If the practitioners agree that death is the best outcome for a patient, the problem arises of how this death is brought about. In recent years the distinction between active and passive euthanasia has formed a significant feature of bio-ethical reflection. It reflects the belief that it is permissible, at least in some cases, to withhold treatment and allow a patient to die when death is imminent, but that it is never acceptable to take any direct action to kill the patient. The important difference between the two is that in passive euthanasia the health-care professional, the doctor, allegedly does nothing to bring about the patient's death. The patient dies not because of the actions of the doctor but because of illness. In contrast, in active euthanasia the doctor does something – for example administers a lethal injection.

This distinction between killing and acts of allowing someone to die is a neat one – perhaps too neat. In fact this distinction needs to be submitted to rigorous scrutiny. The active/passive euthanasia distinction rests on the assumption that killing someone is more ethically reprehensible than letting someone die. But is this case? An example may illustrate the problem.

Frank is married to a wealthy woman called Mary. It is a loveless marriage and Frank decides to do away with his wife. He tampers with the brakes in her car causing her to have a fatal accident. Joe, on the other hand, married a millionaire for her money. He too wants to see the back of her but has not the stomach to kill her. One day he discovers that there is a fault with the brakes of her car. Although he knows she is about to take off on a dangerous road he says nothing, and she is killed in an accident. Frank killed his wife but Joe 'simply' let her die. In ethical terms did either husband act more responsibly? Both acted out of the same motive, personal gain, and both had exactly the same end in view.

Of course the comparison between these situations and euthanasia is in some respects an unfair one, since doctors are not prompted by personal gain in the same way. They are concerned with cases in which terminally patients are facing horrific suffering. None the less, is there all that much difference between letting a patient die, for humane reasons, and giving a patient a lethal injection for humane reasons? The American Medical Association identified the crucial issue as 'the intentional termination of the life of one human by another'. The document went on to deny that the cessation of treatment represents the intentional termination of life. Yet for what other reason does a doctor stop treating a patient if not for terminating life? I wish to defend the view that intentionally ceasing life-prolonging treatment is the intentional termination of life, because the doctor foresees that by ceasing treatment the patient will die. The core of the argument is that in passive euthanasia doctors are not exactly doing nothing – they are consciously letting a patient die.

This is not to cast any aspersions on the doctors involved. In very many cases the decision to withdraw treatment is not made by the doctors, but by the patients themselves or their guardians. Patients have the right to refuse treatment – even, as the verdict of some American legal cases suggest, when their reason for refusing treatment is generally agreed to be inadequate. In such circumstances, while doctors can physically prevent the patient's death, they are not free to continue treatment. Therefore, in many cases doctors are not intentionally letting the patient die.

However, justifying passive euthanasia on the grounds that it saves the patient pain and needless suffering opens up a hornet's nest. If one simply withholds treatment, it may take patients longer to die so they may end up suffering much more than if they were given a lethal injection. On this rationale, if it is acceptable to decide not to prolong a patient's suffering by withholding treatment, is it not logical to predicate that active euthanasia is preferable to passive euthanasia? To claim otherwise is to favour the option that causes more suffering than less, and is diametrically opposed to the humanitarian impulse that inspired the decision not to prolong life in the first place. The process of being 'permitted to die' can be slow and painful, whereas being given a lethal injection tends to be quick and painless.

Active euthanasia is often frowned upon because it is considered bad to be the cause of someone's death, since death is perceived as a great evil. If, in a particular case, passive euthanasia is considered acceptable, the presumption is that death is no greater an evil than the patient's continued existence. If this is indeed the case, the usual reason for not wanting to be the cause of someone's death does not hold true. A problem with the debate about active euthanasia to date is that it has been too restricted, that is, limited to a critique of direct attacks on the patient such as a lethal injection. Is turning off a respirator an act of killing or of letting die? What of withholding insulin from a diabetic or antibiotics from a patient with pneumonia?

It may be ethically permissible to cease active treatment, though not so-called 'ordinary care' (though as we shall see this term is unsatisfactory) for patients when that treatment is a burden to them and unlikely to achieve any significant good, even if death may be hastened as a consequence. One approach to this issue is by recourse to the doctrine of 'double effect'. Under this principle, an unhappy result such as death makes an action wrong if it is intended, as in a killing, but it may also arise from an action that is permissible if it is foreseen but not directly intended. Turning off pacemakers, stopping insulin in diabetics, increasing oxygen concentrations in patients with chronic lung disease who require low doses as a stimulus to breathe, failing to monitor appropriate blood levels or treat an infection, may achieve the exact same result as administering a lethal injection.

THE RIGHT TO REFUSE LIFE?

It could be argued that if we accept the right to refuse life-prolonging treatment, then consistency insists that we include patients' right to end their lives, and to obtain help in doing so. In this perspective a patient's right to refuse treatment implies a right to voluntary euthanasia. Some legal writers view the right to refuse treatment as an example of the right to privacy or as 'the right to bodily self-determination'. Accordingly, one has the right to decide what happens to one's own body, and the right to refuse treatment is an example of that right. But if one has the right to determine what happens to one's own body, then should one not have the right to choose to end one's life, and a right to receive help to do so?

However, the right to refuse treatment is not the same as, nor does it include, a right to voluntary euthanasia, even if both stem from the right to bodily self-determination. The right to refuse treatment does not constitute a 'right to die', even though one may freely choose to exercise this right even at the risk of death. The right to refuse medical treatment ensures that a patient is protected from the unwanted interferences of others. It does not mean that a person has a right to decide whether to live or die. The inevitable logic of voluntary euthanasia is that people have the right not merely to be left alone, but also the right to be killed.

Proponents of active euthanasia for example sometimes link their campaign with a demand for the right to suicide. The case against the legalising of suicide rests on three planks:

1. The concern to nurture the care of dying patients will

not be served by emphasis on suicide as an option.

2. The trust relationship of patients with doctors is not enhanced with the introduction of measures to allow practitioners to assist suicide.

3. Legislation is an intrusion into value-laden and extremely complex medical decisions that are more appropriately dealt with by consultation between patient and practitioner. Law furnishes us with a rich language for reflecting about ethical issues and is a useful vehicle for action as well as talk. But the language of law regularly fails to achieve its desired effect.

One complication in this case is in the treatment of infants. Consent for surgical intrusion normally comes from the parents. As legal guardians, parents are required to provide medical care for their children, and failure to do so can constitute criminal neglect or perhaps even homicide. The courts have in many cases been reluctant to recognise a parental right to terminate life-prolonging treatment. Practitioners who comply with invalid instructions from the parents and permit the infant's death could be liable for criminal prosecution. In such circumstances, doctors are legally bound not to do as the parents wish.

A JEWISH PERSPECTIVE

Different cultures and faith systems approach the active/passive euthanasia debate in very different ways. Judaism, for example, has a very strong antipathy to the idea of active or passive euthanasia. The long established legal-moral system, known as *halacha*, regulates practically all aspects of Jewish life and offers much direction in the area of medical ethics and conduct. In medical decision-making, halacha would consider the 'sanctity of life', the preciousness of every moment, as the foremost issue. As a rule of thumb, preserving life takes precedence over concerns about the quality of life. Jewish law forcefully asserts that life, even that of a terminal, demented, elderly patient is of infinite value; it must be preserved no less than the life of a young and alert child with a hopeful long-term prognosis. This position is conveyed in a classic case where the Mishnah directs that one must immediately remove debris that has fallen upon someone on Shabbat, even though the victim may have very little time to live. Jewish legal codes go a step further and stipulate that he must be saved even though his skull was crushed and he may live for only a few minutes. Even if he is mentally incompetent, for example, his life must be saved. This ruling is based on Judaism's attributing infinite value to human life: 'Infinity being invisible, any fraction of life, however limited its expectancy or its health, remains equally infinite in value.'

An even more dramatic example of this belief is that of a medical emergency in a hospital which has only one working respirator and where this machine is connected to a terminally ill, incompetent 90-year-old. A young motor-accident victim, who will die without the respirator and will probably recover with it, is rushed to the hospital. Halachic authorities decree that the dying elderly patient already on the machine cannot be removed from the respirator. To remove the old man from the respirator would be to imply that the old man's life is less valuable than that of the young one. To pass judgements on the quality of life would, in effect, amount to playing God. Because of a better prognosis for long-term recovery, priority would be given to the young accident victim if the older patient had not already been placed on the respirator. Applying these principles to the clinical setting while there is some debate about whether elderly patients may refuse the initiation of 'tube-feeding', there is widespread agreement that once initiated, it may not be withdrawn.

IN THE INTERESTS OF BALANCE

To reject the term 'passive euthanasia' is not to argue for continued treatment which has little chance of improving the patient's condition and brings greater discomfort than relief. Rather my point has been to show that the active/passive distinction does as much, if not more, to confuse than to clarify and is not an adequate framework to discuss the complexities of ethical questions in the treatment of the terminally ill.

Three

'That There's Cruelty to Animals'

In February 1993 the final judgement made in the House of Lords in the case of *Airedale NHS Trust* v. *Tony Bland* ruled that the attending physicians could legally end any life-sustaining treatment and medical supportive measures designed to keep Mr Bland alive. Mr Bland had lain comatose since sustaining horrific injuries during the Hillsborough football disaster in 1989. The judges highlighted four safeguards which should be observed before discontinuing life-support to a patient in a permanent vegetative state (PVS):

1. Every effort at rehabilitation should be made for at least six months after injury.
2. The diagnosis of irreversible PVS should not be considered confirmed until at least twelve months after injury.
3. The diagnosis should be agreed by at least two other independent doctors.
4. Generally the wishes of the patient's immediate family should be given greater weight.

Lord Goff went on to point out that to discontinue

artificial feeding might be categorised as an omission, which, if deemed to constitute a breach of duty to the patient, is unlawful. However, in the Bland case, he argued that the patient was incapable of swallowing and therefore of eating and drinking in the normal sense of these words. Artificial feeding via a nasogastric tube was therefore a form of life-support, and could be discontinued if treatment was futile and no longer in the best interests of the patient.

What the Bland verdict does *not* do is to give doctors *carte blanche* to withdraw treatment from all patients in a PVS. For the foreseeable future doctors in England and Wales must in each case apply to the High Court for a declaration to determine the legality or otherwise of any proposed discontinuance of life-support, where there is a valid consent on the part of the patient. In addition, a civil court ruling is no guarantee against subsequent prosecution in a criminal court, since a declaration as to the legality or otherwise of future conduct is 'no bar to a criminal prosecution no matter what the authority of the court which grants it'.

In the Tony Bland case, the judge's verdict regarding hydration and nutrition was clearly swayed by the patient's irreversible brain damage, although the law as to killing is unaffected by the victim's mental state. It would be dangerous, though, to extrapolate that verdict to other decisions.

Despite the differences in mental state, pathology and life expectation between a terminally ill sedated patient and one with a PVS, the crucial issue is similar: by withholding fluid and nourishment, in other words the means of sustaining life, is one killing the patient? From a legal point of view the answer could be 'yes'. For some terminally ill patients, especially those who are rendered unable to swallow by heavy sedation, failure to hydrate and nourish artificially could be judged an unlawful omission.

A particular danger of inappropriate sedation arises when carers have reached the limit of their resources. The case of the Winchester rheumatolgist who was convicted of attempted murder demonstrates what can happen when doctor and patient reach the end of their tether.

SETTING LIMITS

Another difficult situation arises when physicians meet for the first time patients who are already demented. An additional complication is that doctors are obliged to consider the interests of society when deciding how much of society's resources to call on in maintaining patients' lives, for example how many tests to order, which conditions to treat, what drugs to use. While most reasonable people would accept that there have to be certain limits, it is much more difficult to establish what these limits are. Advance directives may be helpful, but often they are not specific enough to be meaningful in concrete clinical situations. One example illustrates this fact.

Advances in medical technology render many old directives on the lines of 'I don't want to be hooked up to machines' redundant. Now feeding tubes and medications that come after or in place of the machines can keep patients going for years. Should either of these be withheld because of the wish expressed about machines?

Even if surrogates are named the problems are not solved because problems of interpretation remain. For example if a patient has stated 'I never want to live like a vegetable', should all medication be terminated and her pacemaker turned off if she is pleasantly though not painfully demented in a nursing home?

Doctors find themselves in an invidious situation. On the one hand they are questioned about too little care. On the other they are criticised about too much. They may have to watch interventions which make no sense, for example elderly patients attached to ventilators and restrained in ICU beds because no one can be found to say 'no more'; dying patients who are resuscitated because well-meaning relatives require everything possible be done. One elderly man who saw his demented wife in her ICU bed remarked: 'That there's cruelty to animals.' It sounds repugnant but, given her circumstances, he may well have been right.

AND AT THE HOUR OF OUR DEATH

For many years the provision or withdrawal of artificial nutrition and hydration (ANH) has been a controversial subject, particularly in relation to PVS patients. Why do we persist in the relentless pursuit of artificial nourishment and other treatments to maintain a permanently unconscious existence? In the future, even more than the present, there will be a huge number of PVS patients. Are they to be treated because of an ethical commitment to their humanity, or because of an ethical paralysis in the face of biotechnical progress? The PVS patient is divorced from the normal patterns of human connection and communication, with a life unlike other forms of human existence. Why the struggle to justify terminating a life which, it is argued, has suffered an irreversible loss of consciousness?

According to a recent study of the prognosis of post-traumatic vegetative patients, no patient who remained vegetative beyond three months ever became independent of nursing care. The continued existence of PVS patients is dependent on basic nursing care and on an adequate supply of artificial nutrition and hydration. The reliability of a diagnosis must carry some degree of uncertainty because, thus far, no specific laboratory studies can confirm the clinical diagnosis of PVS. Consequently there is some disagreement as to when a confident diagnosis of PVS can be made. A number of doctors believe a diagnosis can be made after three months without patient improvement, whereas others, such as the American Medical Association (AMA), set a conservative criterion for diagnosis as twelve months of unawareness. Despite the element of doubt, this uncertain clinical experience suggests that extremely few patients who remain vegetative after three months ever recover cognitive functions, and the few who do retain consciousness remain very severely physically and mentally disabled and dependent.

It was the Karen Ann Quinlan case in the 1970s which highlighted the ethical questions about the treatment of PVS patients. All these years later the same questions linger regarding the status of these patients and the definition and determination of death. Three disparate issues need to be considered:

1. The tremendous advances in organ transplantation technology – PVS patients would provide a potential source for scarce organs.
2. The imperative of ensuring a just and fair allocation of scarce resources.
3. Respect for the autonomy and dignity of the PVS patient.

Should the cost of continued health care for the permanently unconscious, or for any patient, be a factor in clinical ethical decision-making? While costs vary, it is an established fact that it is a costly exercise to maintain these patients in a persistent vegetative state. Some economists have argued that an affluent society should feel obliged to meet the costs, whereas an impoverished community must first ensure a just allocation of its scarce health resources. Others argue that in the light of the scarcity of medical resources in wealthy societies, they also cannot afford the costs and must make clinical ethical decisions with due regard for cost-efficiency. In the US alone there are over 5,000 PVS patients – a figure that it has been predicted will increase significantly in the future, especially when the increased longevity of people is considered.

Since the PVS patient can survive for years, even decades, the withdrawal of life-sustaining treatment such as nutritional support may be the cause of death; that is, it is the act of withdrawal that leads to death, not the actual medical condition. One study suggests that the PVS patient experiences nothing. However, the benefits and burdens of continued treatment fall mainly on others. For this reason, some doctors and ethicists have recently argued that decisions about PVS patients should be made with reference to futility.

It is interesting to note that the Hippocratic Corpus encouraged doctors to recognise the limits of medicine: 'to refuse to treat those who are overmastered by their diseases, realising in such cases medicine is powerless.' Serious ethical consequences stem from a practitioner's claim that a particular treatment is futile, particularly in the absence of any degree of consensus about how futility should be determined in practice. The reasons normally advanced for withdrawing treatment – incurable suffering, terminal illness and patient request for withdrawal of life-support treatment – do not apply to PVS patients. The PVS patient is neither dead nor dying, and the withdrawal of ANH is therefore an act of killing.

'HEALTH CARE IS NOT HORTICULTURE'

Those who argue that doctors should be able, at least in some cases, to refuse unilaterally to provide life-support to patients condemned to profoundly diminished lives appeal to one or more of three concerns: futility, cruelty, and wastefulness. Doctors have never been obligated to provide pointless care. They have the authority to cease resuscitation when it is evidently not working, and to refuse to prescribe useless interventions, such as antibiotics for a viral infection.

Medicine's goal is to foster distinctively human life. For this reason it could be argued that life-support for patients in profoundly diminished life is futile either quantitatively, because there is no credible chance of prolonging a reasonable duration of life, or qualitively, because there is no serious possibility of restoring an acceptable quality of life.

The cruelty argument springs from health care's values as a profession: preserving life, curing illness, alleviating suffering, and ameliorating disabilities. Invasive life-support that only prolongs the suffering of the dying is pointless cruelty.

The wastefulness argument starts from the premise that doctors exercise stewardship of approximately 80 per cent of health-care resources in the US, for example, through their power of prescribing, writing orders and influencing patients' choices. Doctors would be ethically irresponsible to employ costly and scarce resources in futile efforts.

It is not to difficult to make a case that, under some definitions of these concepts, doctors are entitled to forswear futile interventions. The problem with this position is that the basic question of whether doctors should be permitted unilaterally to determine whether and when to support patients whose lives are profoundly diminished remains unanswered. It presupposes, rather than establishes, answers to this basic question.

At one end of the spectrum are the vitalists, who argue that all human life is fully valuable, irrespective of the quality. At the other extreme are those who argue that there are some conditions under which a life is no longer of value to the person who has it – that such a person would be better off, or at least no worse off, dead. Accordingly, life is only an instrumental value, a precondition for other goods such as human interaction.

Vitalists have the benefit of one powerful weapon, the threat of litigation. They can seek court orders to compel treatment or allege after the fact that the recalci-trant doctor committed malpractice, abandonment, or even murder. For doctors, the threat of such litigation is formidable because of the potential financial, emotional and professional cost. The very threat of litigation, then, may leave doctors feeling they have no choice but to accede to a patient's or family's demands.

In the context of health care itself, there is a great division between the majority of doctors, for whom the objective of sustaining their patients' lives is instrumen-tal as a means of helping their patients regain or maintain a life that they, the patients, consider worth living, and those physicians who see the preserving of life as an end in itself, regardless of the quality or nature of that end or of their patients' opinions on whether or not the life is worth living.

'Futility' is an emotionally loaded term. It would be more helpful to put the emphasis on benefit: how much benefit for the patient does the proposed management offer? In most western countries determination of futility is left to reasonable medical judgement, and this is the crux of the problem. Doctors frequently disagree on the probability of treatment success, and the goals of treatment. Is the goal of sustaining a biological but unconscious life, in the case of a PVS patient, a reasonable one? Is it always futile to treat the PVS patient? The key issue is not the meaning of futility but whose assessment in a particular case should count. The Institute of Medical Ethics Working Party on the Ethics of Prolonging Life and Assisting Death (1991) urged the medical profession to recognise publicly that withdrawal of artificial nutrition and hydration may be an appropriate way to manage vegetative patients.

The 1983 decision of a California court of appeal in *Barber* v. *Superior Court* was one of the most famous cases in which futility was invoked to support the conclusion that a doctor has no duty to continue treatment 'once it has become futile in the opinion of qualified medical personnel'. The judgement was heavily influenced by the President's Commission for the Study of Ethical Problems in Medicine, and the court defined as futile those procedures that lack the ability to 'improve the prognosis for recovery'.

There are two key questions about a definition of futility. Who will formulate it? Who will apply it?

The definition ought to be framed in terms of patient

outcome. A major problem with the emergence of futility as a central concept in medical decision-making is that the crucial question – 'Futile for what end?' – is apparently unanswered. Legislative efforts in this area have not been satisfactory; for example the state of Georgia defined medical futility as a resuscitative effort that 'will likely be unsuccessful in restoring cardiac and respiratory function or will only restore cardiac and respiratory function for a brief period of time so that the patient will likely experience repeated need for a cardiopulmonary resuscitation over a short period of time'. 'Brief', 'short' and 'likely' all need to be quantified. In cases of unresolved disputes, I would argue for a multidisciplinary ethics committee (including patient representatives) whose verdict would be binding on both parties, rather than a judicial forum, because of the availability of a greater variety of insights and perspectives such a committee will provide.

In an article in *Annals of Internal Medicine* in 1990, Schneiderman *et al.*, defined futility as 'merely preserving permanent unconsciousness or…failing to end total dependence on intensive medical care', both of which are unacceptable ends in health care. However, as we shall see in the following chapter, some people value other outcomes.

Futility becomes ethically unacceptable when it allows doctors unilaterally to decide to limit or cease treatment, based on their own assessments of what outcomes are worth pursuing, without ever affording their patients or patients' surrogates the opportunity to join them in the process of making such decisions. On the other hand we must also recognise that health care must combat premature death, not death itself.

Four

When the Years Are Not Golden

Helga Wanglie was an active, articulate 85-year-old when she tripped over a rug and broke her hip in December 1989. Following her accident, she began lengthy treatment during which her heart gave her a lot of trouble. As a result of her heart problems she spent over a year, from 23 May 1990 until her death on 4 July 1991, lying unconscious in a persistent vegetative state, her breathing maintained by a respirator and her nutrition supplied through a tube.

Such tales of protracted dying have become commonplace in American courtrooms. Judges are frequently requested to approve the decisions of terminally ill patients' next-of-kin to withdraw life-sustaining procedures. It was not surprising that Helga Wanglie's case ended up in the courts. There was a twist in the tale though when her 53-year-old husband refused to consent to the withdrawal of her treatment on the grounds that only God can take a life. Some of the doctors at the Hennepin County Medical Center, where she was a patient, asked a Minnesota district court judge to name another guardian in his place. The judge threw out their action and granted the petition filed by Mr Wanglie, whom the court found to be 'the most suitable and best qualified' of the available guardians. Cases like the Wanglie case are becoming increasingly commonplace.

THE FRAGILE ELDERLY

Many chronically ill patients possess consciousness, however diminished, and are able to feel both pleasure and pain. They are not Karen Quinlans or Tony Blands – their minds have by and large ceased to function but their bodies continue. Such patients are often described as the 'fragile elderly', and opponents of active euthanasia fear they would be targeted if that practice was legalised. Such patients are unable to inform doctors whether they wish to live or die, to be treated or not treated. In many cases they live in institutions where policy and politics dealing with such issues as: criteria for accepting patients, transferring them to the hospital and the withholding of certain treatments shape standards of care.

As the fragile elderly develop medical complications, health-care professionals have to take on the burden of making treatment decisions, or more fundamentally, deciding if they should be treated at all. Institutional policy, family wishes, and legal guidelines will clearly influence the doctor's decisions, but the physicians are not neutral observers. They bring their perceptions of what it means to be a doctor, and of what it means to heal in a situation where 'cure' is an ambiguous term and the answers to treatment choices are not clear. To prolong life and stave off death is a double-edged sword carrying the promise of longevity as well as the shadow of protracted dying. One of the big problems facing old people is that they are very susceptible to paternalistic interventions. Paternalism could lead doctors to refuse to acquiesce in a person's wishes, choices, and actions for that patient's own benefit.

For the first time in human history, the number of elderly outnumbers the number of newborns. A new generation has emerged, the 'old old': persons over 85 years of age, cared for by the elderly over 65 years old. In some instances there are persons over 85 caring for individuals over 100. This will increasingly be the case in the coming years, when many people will be over 100. As a steady stream of reports point out that as the costs of health care will continue to increase during the 90s, greater and greater attention will be focused on limiting those costs by restricting access to health care.

Against this background a number of voices can be heard clamouring for an 'health-care access solution' as the population 'gerifies'. Distributing health-care access on the basis of age conflicts with the inherent ethical principles of medicine and health care, and, for that matter, the principles of justice in society. But what are the alternatives? The public discussion on this issue should focus on the question of what sort of society we ought to be. Have we become so warped that people feel the need to dispatch themselves early in a chronic disease rather than to trust others to care for them? Some disturbing evidence has emerged which suggests that there is a growing trend in elderly suicide. This has been seen as an indication that elderly people feel as threatened by high-technology hospitals where they are stripped of their values at the same time they are stripped of their clothes and put into beds.

Today major ethical and legal issues arise in disputes about certain conditions, such as advanced Alzheimer's disease or a permanent coma, that may or may not be seen as terminal states. Moreover, in the American context, the most expensive form of care is not life-prolonging technology in an acute care setting, but long-term care in a nursing home. It appears that no problem is more complex or more urgent than the formulation of a viable policy of long-term care for the elderly and the chronically disabled.

From a purely utilitarian standpoint, those who contribute nothing to society and drain its resources are disposable. During the Nazi regime two doctors, Binding and Hoche, called such persons 'ballast' existence. In this view, when economic times are prosperous, society does not ask questions about caring for expendable individuals. When times get hard, then such 'ballast existence' must be eliminated. This highlights the danger of linking the rights of vulnerable people with the needs and wants of the wider society. Nazi doctors transformed their social backdrop into a euthanasia factor. This is unacceptable ethically and politically, since it is an assault on the principle of respecting individual wishes, and of respecting persons themselves.

In 1986 former governor Lamm of Colorado was reported as saying (though he denied saying it) that old people have a duty to die and get out of the way. The following year, though, in a major speech, he offered as the ninth of his 'Ten commandments of an ageing society' the following premise: 'Do not let young children suffer because of health care we give the elderly.' Essentially Lamm's proposal was designed to curtail spending on the aged on the basis of a utilitarian social policy. In this perspective the increasing gerification of society makes cut-offs essential. Since the greatest good of the greatest number requires that other social goods go to the workers and children who provide for the future and for the care of the elderly, ageist criteria should be used.

Lamm wages a war against what he terms 'anti-social ethics'. This is an ethics of emotional appeal to caring for the elderly. While sounding lofty, it actually punishes society. In his view it is a grossly irresponsible allocation of resources to finance machines and techniques which soak up a lot of resources but yield limited results. Since considerable costs in caring for the elderly are borne by the government, it is not surprising that Lamm targeted the aged in his proposals. Moreover, the elderly use a disproportionate share of health-care costs compared to other members of society. Limits on their care would have more immediate impact in terms of utilitarian policy than cut-offs with other groups.

How is this situation of expensive treatment for the elderly to be resolved? One possibility is by recourse to quality-of-life judgements which allow us to stop certain kinds of treatment for incompetent patients, but at the risk of capriciousness, manipulation, and lack of respect for persons. At the other end of the spectrum a civil-rights model institutionally embodied in an impartial committee mechanism is more likely to achieve errors of possibly unnecessary and generally costly treatment. In between we require a set of ethical judgements which include key principles such as equity, decency, individual rights, and the limits of state authority.

Norman Daniels in his books *Just Health Care*, and

Am I My Parent's Keeper? argues that a prospective national policy, in which citizens decide ahead of time that certain technologies would be denied for all at a specified age, would be a just method for allocating resources. This is called a 'prudential plan model', since each person would then plan for the future knowing exactly what to expect. This model draws heavily on John Rawls's notion of a 'veil of ignorance'. If everyone were 'ignorant' about their future health and economic status, then prudent people would select a scheme that would improve their chances of reaching a normal life span over one that would reduce their chances of reaching a normal life span but improve their chances once a normal life span had been achieved.

Another variation of a health-care rationing model which uses age as cut-off point would provide priority claims to health-care resources in inverse proportion to people's chronological age. Rationing would not necessarily be done on the basis of age, but instead on the basis of priorities. As persons age, they have already used some of their social power to compete for goods and services and have less claim than others on future resources.

Rationing approaches generally share five important beliefs:

1. rationing of health-care is essential;
2. such rationing should concentrate on less effective, more expensive forms of care;
3. even though rationing will occur, it should not impede social support for or the quality of life of the aged;
4. all people should know ahead of time what

   categories of care will and will not be available to
   them at various stages of their life span;
5. intergenerational justice and altruism should be
   served in allocative decisions.

While these ageist proposals have therefore some
merits, they open up an ethical can of worms. Firstly,
even with the best-laid plans, people cannot be held
responsible for illnesses they contract, especially later in
life. For this reason people must be treated in an
individual manner. While it makes sense to seek to curb
spending on high-technology medicine, most of the
spending by the aged and their families is for chronic
care and nursing-home care.
   Secondly, rationing based on a 'natural life span' is
difficult to defend in modern, developed societies.
How are we to treat the many patients over 80 or 85?
Some patients are operated on when they are over 100
years old and do well. Perhaps the biggest weakness
of ageist proposals is that they fail adequately to
consider that physiological age correlates poorly with
chronological age – as a number of research projects,
for example the Baltimore Longitudinal Study,
suggest. For this reason age is a very poor criterion for
judging who should and who should not receive life-
prolonging technology. While advocates of rationing
claim to protect the intrinsic value of human life once
factors such as the social welfare of all, economics, or a
national health policy that limits treatment on the basis
of a natural life span, are used to allocate care, the
intrinsic value of individuals is at risk. One
commentator described such rationing emotively as
'abortion at the other end'.

A PEACEFUL DEATH?

Daniel Callahan, frequently described as America's foremost medical ethicist, argues that in recent decades bio-ethical discussions on death and dying have been devoted to law and regulation, rather than to the place and meaning of death in human life. In his *The Troubled Dream of Life: Living with Mortality* (1993) (the book can be seen as the final part of a trilogy which began with *Setting Limits* (1987) and *What Kind of Life?* (1990)) – he attempts to bring the legal and policy issues back into closer contact with 'some of the oldest questions of human existence', for example what kind of person should we try to become as we approach the end of our lives? What kind of stance toward death should we, as patients, doctors and members of the human community, adopt?

Callahan argues that a desire for control should be balanced by a willingness to accept the inevitable, since death is an essential part of biological nature and not an evil to be fought at all costs. Moreover, the fact that death has become a problem reflects our mistaken views about nature and human responsibility. Our goal should not be endlessly to prolong life through medical intervention, but rather to ask ourselves how we can use the possibilities of medical technology in order to achieve a peaceful death.

Callahan takes from the French historian Ariés a distinction between the 'tame' and 'the wild' death, that is, a death within the natural part of the cycle of life, and the death of technological medicine. Although we seem to cherish the notion that death must have been worse in former times, in fact people accepted death more calmly and did in fact die over a relatively short period of time. In recent years death has been transformed in the hands of modern health care and as a consequence ethical discussion has tended to focus on individual rights. The problem with this debate is that it asks the wrong question: have we a right to choose to die rather than what kind of death should we pursue? He contends that instead of pushing the limits of life extension as far as possible, health care should be devoted to the management of death in order to achieve what he refers to as a 'peaceful death'.

In this perspective, health care distorts our understanding of nature since doctors see death almost as a correctable biological inadequacy. In the effort to master mortality, death is no longer an inevitable part of biological nature, but the result of human actions or decisions. The crucial ethical distinction between human acts and acts of nature has become blurred. Death is no longer understood as an inevitable natural event that eludes human control. Now many see it as an ethical obligation to use all medical means available to combat death. A perversion has taken place in which death has moved out of the realm of nature into the realm of human responsibility. The essential difference between a peaceful death, as advocated by Callahan, and a tame death, as described by Ariés, lies in the fact that technological advances allow for the management of time and circumstances of death. A peaceful death complements the advantages of the tame death with the technological improvements of contemporary death.

While Callahan correctly points out that doctors must be held accountable if they fail to administer proper treatment, he also stresses that if the doctor, in a well-considered manner, stops treating the patient, the patient's death is not caused by the fatal disease. He goes on to distinguish between *causality*, that is, the impersonal, independent forces of biological nature, and *culpability*, that is, eg the responsibility of human beings for their actions. In the absence of this distinction, everything that happens can be attributed to human agency. Death becomes the result of human choices and not the independent workings of nature. Nature gets swallowed up in the medical realm. At its starkest: where nature was, human choice is. Where choice is, technology is. And where technology is, choice is transformed. While clearly we ought not to return to pre-modern conceptions of nature we require a plausible and positive interpretation of nature, one free of the conceit that nature has disappeared.

Callahan seeks to invoke an image of the self that is more flexible, less manipulative, more interdependent with others, a self that will choose its stance toward nature rather than trying to dominate it. In this respect the self is able to give meaning to unavoidable suffering as a part of meaningful life and a decline in our ability to manipulate and control does not imply a loss of dignity. Instead, our dignity derives from the way we come to understand and master this decline, and from the stance we adopt towards it. Callahan puts considerable stress on the fact that the aim to master one's dying is not the same as the aim to control it – mastering death is mastering the self in the face of death. On the other hand, aiming at total control is doomed to lead to the loss of mastery of the self. Such a self has become dependent upon medical technology.

A striking metaphor is used by Callahan to express his ideas on personhood and mortality. He compares the art of medicine with the art of the sculptor. In the same way the sculptor can harm the stone by ignoring its innate characteristics, so health care can harm death by ignoring biological restraints. Health care must seek to enhance life, but not at the cost of deforming death.

This leads him to pose the question 'Of each serious illness – especially with the elderly – a question should be asked and a possibility entertained: could it be that this illness is the one that either will be fatal, or – since some disease must be fatal – should soon be allowed to be fatal?' This question is based on the belief that this death now may be better than another death later. Callahan argues that we must abandon the current policy of 'when in doubt, treat' that is, treating each potentially fatal illness as if it *must* be reversed. Since so many patients have a chronic illness, we need a health-care system that accepts its own limitations, both biological and financial; that stresses quality of life rather than the length of life, and that allows for a low-cost, non-technological death.

Unlimited technological progress cannot be afforded nor defended: 'Some limits must be set, limits that may make it perfectly clear in advance just who will not receive potentially life-saving treatment.' Accordingly, society should seek a consensus about priorities. We cannot allow an unlimited amount of money to be spent on individual cases at the neglect of public health. Futile or marginally useful care must be avoided. To prevent subjective decisions, standards for passing futility assessments should be developed collectively rather than with individual patients on a case-by-case basis. Callahan suggests this might best be done in individual hospitals 'where joint medical–lay panels could help to establish an institutional policy sensitive to local needs and values' in order to allow consensual norms and publicly visible policies to develop. In the course of time, unlimited patient choice would yield to general societal standards.

Callahan steers into more shaky ground when he argues that the management of death should not consume an undue share of resources. Does the term 'undue' not do more to confuse than to clarify? Even more contentious is Callahan's assertion that apart from ethical and medical reasons, a treatment can be considered futile because in the light of resource limitations it must be considered economically unjustifiable. Does not this position give too much importance to the economic dimension – with the economic on at least a par with the ethical?

Perhaps in the high-tech world of modern health care, what is most needed is a retrieval of the ancient Greek ideal which enjoined on doctors that the time to stop treatment lay in a balance between the art of medicine and nature with which it must work. Callahan makes a valuable contribution to the debate by retrieving in a critical way (in marked contrast to the way 'nature' has been bandied around in a casual, narrow, uncritical way in the past) the ethical significance of nature. However, Callahan's position leaves many unanswered questions.

What of the case of an Alzheimer's patient who, in the early stages of the disease and still competent, writes an advance directive (we shall be returning to advance directives in much greater detail in a subsequent chapter) rejecting life-sustaining treatment in the event of a life-threatening illness, but who, in the later stages of the disease and no longer competent, continues to enjoy living? When the Alzheimer's reaches a life-threatening situation, should the advance directive be respected? One of the most forceful arguments for rejecting the advance directive in such cases is provided by Ronald Dworkin in a recent work, *Life's Domain*. His essential thesis is that patients have an interest in integrity and that dying in certain ways may be incompatible with the overall integrity of the person. In this perspective, an extremely independent person may suffer a loss of integrity by dying in a manner involving great dependency on others.

I welcome Dworkin's emphasis on integrity as a helpful contribution to the debate. However, I wish to defend the view that integrity provides justification for ignoring the patient's advance directive in certain circumstances. Firstly, having integrity involves living a principled life. The 'demented' person's integrity is not threatened in this sense by wishing to continue living, because she or he is incompetent and therefore cannot violate the principles which formerly governed her or his life. Keeping the person alive does not threaten this sense of integrity. Secondly, integrity also relates to living a coherent life in which a person's desires, values, and character traits are integrated to form a coherent whole. The Alzheimer's patient who enjoys life may be highly integrated, in that she or he has simple and coherent desires. It is when failure to implement the directive would violate the patient's principles that a serious assault on integrity is caused. The crucial issue is whether the values expressed in the patient's rejected advance directive are no longer the patient's values. If so, integrity provides no valid reason for believing that those values should be forced on the patient.

A third relevant consideration is the doctor's sense of integrity. Those who refuse to treat so-called demented patients desiring treatment may find it difficult to maintain their own integrity because of the danger of violating long-held professional principles to which they are committed.

BASIC INSTINCT

Two fears seem to compete with each other among the elderly. On the one hand, they fear that they will be abandoned or neglected if they became critically ill or begin to die and that few will care about their fate: on the other hand, they worry that they will be excessively treated and their lives painfully extended. One commentator claims that doctors are practising in an age of 'cognitive dissonance'. Their basic instinct is to treat and cure the sick, but they are unsure of what to do for those who are neither curable nor dying. As a norm they provide minimal care, treating simple illness with standard care, and forgo technologically more complex or intrusive care. Treatment is not necessarily an all-or-nothing decision. Treatment options can be stratified on a number of levels. There are scales of intrusiveness, scales of risk, levels of technological complexity. However, major problems emerge when fundamental life-and-death decisions have to be taken. Is a patient who no longer knows who she or he is better off dead or alive?

What is routine treatment for a patient with pneumonia may not be ethically required if the patient also suffers from terminal cancer and if the treatment would only prolong the dying process. If the treatment has no reasonable prospect of benefiting the patient, it is optional in ethical terms. Likewise, if the burdens, for example the suffering caused by the chemotherapy, outweigh the probable benefits, perhaps extension of life by a month, the treatment is optional. No single treatment can always be considered as obligatory or optional; depending on the medical circumstances, the use of a respirator or intravenous feeding may be obligatory or optional.

Health care must combat premature death, not death in itself. Medicine is the science of care, not the science of cure, and in caring, health-care professionals must suffer themselves. Such difficult experiences are part of the fabric of health care that bring compassionate people to the profession, not drive them away. Health care should strive to alleviate human suffering, but that is not to imply that its function is to find a quick and easy way to end the lives of those doctors think have a 'futile' life.

A LAST RESTING PLACE

One of the most encouraging developments in recent years in the treatment of the aged has been the flourishing of the hospice movement on a global basis, a development which has done much to take the mystery and fear out of death and dying. While it is not possible for the hospice movement to change the essential character of death, it has done a lot to allay people's fears. Under the influence of hospice movements of western medicine, Japanese society, for example, has shown great interest in terminal care and hospice movements. However, some Japanese are arguing that hospices adapted to the Japanese cultural climate are necessary. One Buddhist hospice was established and called *Vihara*, which means the house for rest and care in Sanskrit. This raises the question of whether we think of death as an event which occurs during a specific moment in time or as a process. Although the idea of death as a process is supported by a number of ethicists, it is the hospice movement which takes this viewpoint most forcibly. Its concern is to improve the quality of life within the process rather than simply to lengthen it. Traditionally we have spoken of a quality of living; now is the time for us to also concentrate on a 'quality of dying'.

Five

Suffer Not the Little Children

In November 1981 a noted paediatrician, the late Dr Leonard Arthur, was acquitted of the attempted murder of a newborn baby, John Pearson. The child had Down's Syndrome, and when the infant was rejected by his mother, the doctor had prescribed dihydrocodeine and 'nursing care only'. Proceedings against Dr Arthur were initiated by the Life organisation on the basis that it was morally evil to deny an innocent human being reasonably straightforward protection against life-threatening conditions.

The defence argued that the doctor's primary duty is to relieve, prevent, or minimise patients' pain and suffering – while doctors must not kill patients they are not obliged, in all circumstances, to prevent their patients dying. In certain cases babies are born with such severe physical and or mental disadvantage that medical intervention to increase the baby's chances of survival is not clearly justified. Such lives, if they are to be maintained, are likely to be disabled to a considerable and sometimes very severe degree, and their chances of ordinary human flourishing are low. Also they are likely to impose a great burden of care on their parents or on the community if their parents reject them or die, and other members of the family may be adversely and severely affected by this burden. For these reasons doctors may in good conscience let severely disabled young infants die when their parents are opposed to or do not wish for life-saving medical intervention. The verdict left many unanswered questions.

SEEN BUT NOT HEARD?

Such have been the advances in medicine that doctors can cause the prolongation of the life of seriously deformed children who in previous times would have died young. In such a situation it is not clear that life so prolonged is good for the child. Ethical issues involving decisions about euthanasia and young children (it is difficult to arrive at a universally acceptable definition of young children) differ substantially from those relating to adult euthanasia. The difference lies in the obvious fact that infants and young children are unable to make decisions about their own futures and in this respect are not the autonomous ethical agents that adults are. While adults usually decide their own fate, others make the decisions for young children. Accordingly, the ethical issues in aiding the death of young children involve a wide spectrum of issues in relation to the rights of children, the status of parental rights, the obligations of parents to prevent the suffering of their children, and the possible implications for society of allowing or expediting the death of seriously defective infants.

In the treatment of adults facing imminent death, decisions are made on the basis that people have the right to refuse treatment, and such a choice can be said to be an affirmation of the rationality and autonomy of the self. In legal terms adults are *sui uris* – they are responsible for their actions. However, infants or young children are unable to make decisions for themselves. Others must take responsibility for them and act on their behalf. They live in and through the care of those who are responsible for them, and those responsible for them exercise the infants' rights on their behalf. Children exist in and through their families and society.

For these reasons, treating infants with respect has a qualitative difference from treating adults with respect. It is not possible to respect either a newborn infant's or a very young child's autonomy. The rights of the infant are exercised and 'held in trust' by others until the child is able to make autonomous decisions.

Medical judgements about whether or not to treat a young child – for instance, letting anencephalic children, who congenitally lack all or most of the brain, die – often hinge on the probability and cost of attaining such autonomy. It is important to establish at the outset that when speaking of 'cost' in the treatment of small children, we are not just speaking about money, but also the stress and trauma that lengthy and uncertain treatment of the child could cause the parents.

This in turn highlights the issue of the obligations of parents when the chances of their child having a full human life is remote. The medical and parental assessment should be animated by the expected lifestyle and the cost of its attainment. The decision about treatment belongs to them in a way that it does not belong to anyone else, including the child itself. The nurturing of the child falls to the parents, and when considerable cost and little prospect of reasonable success are present, the parents may conclude that life-prolonging treatment is not appropriate.

In such circumstances the doctor's role is to present sufficient information in 'parent friendly' language to assist them in reaching a decision. The critical issues to be determined are:

- Has the child any reasonable prospect of a decent quality of life?
- What would be the cost to the family of lengthy treatment?
- What would be the cost to society?

MONEY, MONEY, MONEY

A more problematic situation arises when the expected future quality of life would be of normal quality, though its attainment would be very costly in human and financial terms. Should high costs themselves be an adequate reason to discontinue lengthy treatment? As a norm, that decision would be left to the parents. However, society would intervene in cases where parents have neglected their children in such a way as to undermine and respect their care or where intervention would prevent infants from needless suffering. For example, hospital personnel could seek an injunction to force treatment of the child in the absence of parental consent. The health-care professional equipped with the facts of the case becomes the natural advocate of the child when the parents are apparently negligent.

Yet further complications are caused by the cases of infants where some prospects for normal intelligence and a fair lifestyle do exist, but where these chances are remote and their realisation expensive. How improbable does the prospect of a good life have to be in order not to be worth great pain and disease? Again we return to the costs to the parents and society; prolonging life would not be appropriate when not only is there not only little likelihood of full human life, but also a certainty of great suffering, to patient and family, if the life is prolonged. The role of the health-care professional is not to prolong life at all costs. One recent case raised a lot of ethical questions in this area.

THE LAURA DAVIES CASE

The tragic story of the multiple transplant patient, five-year-old Laura Davies, who died in November 1993, attracted much attention. Laura was born with gastroschesis, a condition affecting ten to twenty children a year in Britain, and in which normal eating is impossible because the intestine is a fraction of its usual length. Victims are fed intravenously, and most die as other organs break down. By the age of three, Laura's liver had failed. In 1992 she had a successful operation, and received a new bowel and liver, but hers was to be a short-lived recovery. In the summer of '93 she developed growths on her new bowel, and other organs were starting to fail. She could not eat and was losing weight. Her only hope of survival was a liver and bowel transplant, with such pioneering surgery being offered by the team in Pittsburgh.

Her final operation in Pittsburgh Children's Hospital involved the transplant of six organs – a procedure requiring the powerful immunosuppressive drug FK506. The drug suppressed Laura's immune system and as a consequence reduced the doctors' ability to recognise abnormal cells. When Laura had a stroke, her parents, not wanting her to suffer any more even though the hospital was prepared to continue treatment, decided that the mechanical ventilation system keeping her alive should be switched off. By that time their daughter's body had been invaded by a proliferation of small cancer-like growths. These growths, started by the common Epstein-Barr virus, are known as lympho-proliferative disease.

Apart from the human tragedy of Laura's death and the painful saga of drips, drugs, transplants, cancer and death, there are a number of thorny ethical issues arising from the case – particularly following claims by Laura's parents immediately after her death that they did not receive all the relevant information about the possible side-effects of the drugs administered after the operation. It is probable that if such was the case, it was the product of a misunderstanding at a time of immense emotional stress rather than a deliberate omission. Even so, if this misunderstanding did arise it makes a mockery of the principle of informed consent which we discussed in the last chapter.

A second problem is whether or not Laura's parents were right in ordering that the ventilation should be shut off, particularly as the team at the hospital was prepared to continue treatment. As in the case of the Hillsborough victim, Tony Bland, it once more highlights the ambiguity about borderline cases between life and death. It also raises questions about treatment options. If a procedure offers a palpable chance of life, or of postponing death, it is difficult to say it should not be offered. In advanced surgery, the success rate will always be below 100 per cent, but does that make it ethically irresponsible to attempt it?

Another problem was the sheer scale of the experimental treatment which Laura was subjected to: the transplant of six organs in one operation alone. It has been suggested that this course of treatment served the interests of scientific research but not the best interests of the patient.

Historically, experimental medicine has been something of a minefield. In the Western world the Hippocratic tradition has always emphasised the principle *primum non nocere* (first do no harm). In other words, the interests of the patient must always prevail over the interests of society. The World Medical Association's 1975 declaration on the subject reiterated that sentiment. However, in practice ethical decisions in medicine are much hazier; the good of the patient is not an end in itself. There could not have been the advances in such areas as chemotherapy and kidney transplants if health-care professionals had not taken account of possible benefits to future patients. How, though, are doctors to strike the correct balance between the interests of the individual patient and the good of society? What constraints should there be on doctors working in this area? How much risk should a patient be reasonably expected to face? Should experimental techniques be turned to only as a last resort, or much earlier if they offer a reasonable chance of life to the patient?

A complicating factor in judging the wisdom of experimental techniques is that they are generally used when all else has failed. The patients to whom they are applied are likely to have been ill for longer and to have a smaller chance of recovery. New procedures should not necessarily be dismissed because of the failure of an individual to respond to them successfully. It is worth noting that at the time of Laura's death, eight of the twelve multi-organ patients treated by her surgeon were still alive. Charges that Laura's treatment was irresponsible must be made with reference against this background of comparative success.

The NHS refused to pay for Laura's (or similar cases) transplants and for expensive life-long anti-rejection drugs. Laura's case was taken up by the media. Her photogenic face and engaging personality stirred the hearts of the British public, and a huge sum of money was raised. Moreover, she had the advantage of having a wealthy benefactor, King Fahd of Saudi Arabia, who provided substantial financial resources for her treatment.

In Laura's case, the first transplant was relatively uncontroversial, but the second raised more difficult issues. The organs she was given could instead have been given to another child, or two or three other children, who might have stood a better chance of survival. Moreover, the estimated £1,000,000 sterling cost of the treatment could have saved hundreds of children if invested in vaccination programmes in Africa, or tens if spent in intensive-care units in West. Asked for her opinion, Baroness Warnock, chairperson of the commission into research on human embryos, commented: 'Such surgery is always a waste of money. Anyone with that sort of money would do better to give it to something with a realistic chance of success.'

Treatments will be determined by the parents' success or failure in the charity lottery. The ethics of media campaigns which raise a lot of money for expensive treatment for a tiny minority of children, when so many other needy children are left unaided, also need to be questioned. Laura's face was a portrait of mesmeric innocence and touched a chord with many people. If she had not been so photogenic and 'media-friendly', would the media have taken on her case so assiduously? Laura's case and her parents' suffering were the subject of constant media monitoring. Is it ethically responsible to devote so much press space and prime radio and TV news time to the life and death of one child, when so many other children who require expensive treatment are ignored by the media?

The Laura Davies controversy underlines the need for a sustained and vigorous public debate on the ethics of treating terminally ill children. It is a sobering statistic that 40,000 children die in the world every day. According to UNICEF, 25,000 of them die from preventable diseases, and 8,000 of those from not being vaccinated. Should resources be spent on exotic treatment for an elite few or on primary health care for the many?

Keeping aloof ultimately involves complicity. The time has come for health-care professionals and ethicists to come together to articulate a conceptual framework in which allocative decisions in general and new ethical questions in general medicine can be boldly and honestly confronted. No prescription needs to be written more urgently.

Contemporary society displays a proliferation of many interests, individual, social, environmental and medical, each demanding a fair share of society's scarce resources. Unfortunately, there are not enough resources available to meet all those needs. There is no easy ethical blueprint to which society can refer to establish that all of its obligations have been justly discharged. In the context of difficult decisions about the distribution of resources in health care, two difficult questions are raised. How is the tension between the rights of individual patients and the overall good of society to be resolved? What are the relevant inequalities that justify giving more of the scarce resources to some potential patients and less to others?

The two criteria which I suggest as important points of reference are *the need for health care* and *the equality of patients*. Other important considerations are that the poorer sections of society, or those with special problems, such as the disabled, should receive special attention. They should receive favoured treatment in public policy and from all engaged in the delivery of health-care. However, the very complexity of these issues underlies the importance of a sustained and vigorous debate on the ethical aspects of policies in the distribution of scarce health resources.

One commentator contends that there is a 'family commons', consisting of limited, private resources on which families depend to survive and function. He claims that we should allow families to refuse treatment for defective newborns who would put great strain on their emotional and financial resources. There are occasions when a choice must be made between the well-being of the unfortunate and that of others in competition for limited resources. Accordingly, he goes on to suggest that by direct or proxy decision, it may be reasonable at times to make a tragic choice of neglect, even death, for one, in order to protect others. What this position fails to consider is that there may be less drastic alternatives, such as having the baby adopted.

In situations involving 'defective babies', it might be argued that no 'reasonable' person would want to be kept alive under those circumstances. Efforts to formulate satisfactory criteria of 'quality of life' or 'meaningful life' have been unsuccessful. Standards of

'quality of life' or 'meaningful life' require protection
from subjective judgements of social worth, for example
a tendency to define quality of life in terms of produc-
tivity. One study has suggested that doctors are inclined
to treat patients with neurological and mental difficulties less vigorously than patients with physical difficulties. Another criteria suggested is 'humanhood'. This
term is suspect because it is framed in terms of a
patient's standard of utility or social worth, that is, the
individual's potential contribution to society.

However, to use the term 'quality of life' is fraught
with pitfalls, since it shifts the question from whether
treatments are beneficial to patients to whether patients'
lives are beneficial to themselves. Such an approach
could pave the way for a more relaxed attitude to so-
called 'active' or 'involuntary' euthanasia. This danger
is evident in cases such as that of the American, Earle
Spring, a 78-year-old man who suffered from senility
and chronic kidney failure. As a result of his senility he
was in a nursing home, and because of his chronic
kidney failure, he required dialysis. Although he had
indicated to nurses that he did not want to die, his wife
and son sought court approval to remove him from
dialysis so that he could die. The Massachusetts
Supreme Court approved this request – apparently on
'quality-of-life' considerations. This suggests that terms
such as 'quality of life' or 'meaningful life' are too loose
and vague, too susceptible to corruption by judgements
of social worth, and too easily directed against the
senile and severely mentally disabled.

NAHKIRA'S DEATH

One possible way forward might be to replace such
slogans with the term 'the patient's best interests'. Such

a shift does not end the problem, because clearly the criteria of 'the patient's best interests' are not evident. Efforts to provide more protection for incompetent patients by reducing discretion may well backfire if they are so restrictive they simply swing the pendulum to the opposite extreme.

In November 1994 another English case highlighted the dangers of possible abuses of parents acting on a 'patient's best interests' rationale. A couple found guilty of manslaughter after refusing life-saving treatment for their nine-year-old diabetic daughter lost their appeals against conviction and sentence. Dwight Harris, a Rastafarian, 'clearly and deliberately' went against the advice of his GP and hospital doctors before 'emaciated' Nahkira died in hospital from a diabetic coma, said Lord Justice Kennedy in the Court of Appeal. He went on to add: 'Not only did he go against the advice, but in reality he must have watched that child waste – and society demands that an effective and indeed realistic sentence be passed against an appellant who behaves in that way.'

The court upheld the conviction and two-and-a-half-year prison sentence imposed on Harris at Nottingham Crown Court in November the previous year by Mr Justice Tucker, who had described him as a 'zealot' for refusing to allow hospital staff to give Nahkira insulin because of religious beliefs. Lord Kennedy ruled the trial judge's summing-up to the jury had been 'impeccable' and the conviction could not be faulted. He also dismissed appeals by Harris's wife against her conviction and eighteen-month suspended sentence. The trial judge said that she had been subject to her husband's stubborn will.

FAMILY MATTERS

While it is not ethically acceptable to kill patients or to let patients die for the sake of others, it is sometimes justifiable to keep them alive even against their wishes for the sake of others, for example, a child's need for a mother. Such verdicts must meet a heavy burden of proof. Paul Ramsey argues that decisions about whether and which treatment ought to be provided really depend on objective 'medical indications'. His belief is that doctors as agents should make such judgements about patients in the context of their own commitment to care for and preserve life, rather than to serve patients' wishes. The practitioners' decisions should be based on medical factors that are objective, even though they cannot be determined free from the possibility of error. Even for conscious, competent patients, he does not stress the 'right of refusal' but instead a right to 'participate' in medical decisions that affect them. Accordingly, health-care professionals have priority in decisions regarding incompetent patients because the primary factors are medical rather than valuational.

However, if we consider that the question of whether and which treatment ought to be provided depends on an evaluation of the patient's condition, including their best interests, we should give priority to the family, because of their presumed familiarity with and presumed identification with the patient's values. Since these decisions are valuative, it is inappropriate to remove them from the family. This is not to suggest that the priority of the family is final. If health-care professionals believe that a familial decision to cease treatment is against a patient's best interests, they should try to persuade the family members to change their minds. If necessary, they should appeal to the courts, because it is not their function simply to provide information and withdraw, acquiescing in familial decisions which they believe goes against the patient's best interests. Otherwise they are simply technicians and not ethical agents. Another problem for the doctors in dealing with terminally ill children is how much information to give the parents – particularly when the parents are very upset.

THE DOCTOR'S DILEMMA

In 1957 Dr Maurice Davidson began his chapter on truth-telling in a book on medical ethics with the following quotation from the book of Ecclesiastes: 'In much wisdom is much grief: and he that increaseth knowledge increaseth sorrow.' This highlights the human dilemmas doctors face in breaking distressing news to the already traumatised next-of-kin of patients.

Sissela Bok, in her book *Lying* (1978), considers three major arguments which are said to justify deception in health care in the context of fatal or grave disease, or in informing patients of the risks of treatment or research. Firstly, doctors' Hippocratic obligations to benefit and not harm their patients override any requirements of not deceiving people. On this line of reasoning, patients who are seriously ill already have sufficient problems, so why increase them by giving patients distressing news – particularly as patients' prospects of recovery often depend crucially on their morale? Passing on unpleasant medical information could possibly undermine these and consequently damage patients' prospects of recovery. Secondly, it is argued, with some justification, that doctors are rarely, or never, in a position to know the truth, since they can never be sure of the diagnosis or prognosis. Moreover, even if patients were told the truth, they would rarely, if ever, be in a position to understand it. Thirdly, it is sometimes claimed that patients do not wish to be told the truth when it is dire, particularly when they have a dangerous or fatal condition.

The principal problem with these approaches is that they show scant regard for patient autonomy – which forms a central part of the doctor–patient relationship. Deception in medical contexts almost certainly involves denying patients adequate information for rational deliberation. Even from a utilitarian viewpoint, it is probably ethically suspect unless there is a compelling reason to believe that in a particular case overall welfare would be enhanced by deception.

In this situation, the best judges of whether or not knowing the truth about difficult facts will or will not improve their welfare are the patients themselves. Clearly this is poses a major practical problem: how can the physician discover a patient's opinions without disclosing any unpleasant facts to those patients who would prefer to know such information? There is no easy answer. For some patients the most effective weapon may be denial. This may be established by sensitive questioning – a process which is very time consuming for doctors.

Dr Pat O'Shea, in his Clint Eastwood-inspired title *A Fistful of Doctors* (1991), had some pertinent words of criticism for his colleagues in the medical profession:

'Hurry' is the commonest sin committed by modern general practitioners. Morning surgeries, afternoon surgeries, evening surgeries, Saturday surgeries, Sunday surgeries. For the patient, plenty of surgeries but very little time...Patients pay for our expertise. Do they not also pay for our time?'

The comments are addressed to GPs but they have a wider application in the medical profession – particularly in dealing with children and their parents.

Six

The Long Arm of the Law

In 1988, in the case of Nancy Beth Cruzan, the Supreme Court in Missouri was asked to declare a constitutional right to die. Ms Cruzan had lain in a persistent vegetative state without hope of recovery since a car accident in January 1983, her life maintained by artificial nutrition and hydration. Convinced their daughter would not wish to continue to live in such conditions her parents sought to end her tube-feeding. Not only did the court say no; it also set a high standard of evidence for withdrawing treatment, claiming that her guardians could not exercise her right to refuse treatment for her, and that the state's 'unqualified' interest in preserving life should prevail. Two years later, the case was considered by the US Supreme Court, the first of more than fifty 'right to die' cases considered by state courts since 1976 to be heard there. Ms Cruzan had indicated that she would not have wished to continue her life if she could not live 'halfway normally'. On a number of occasions she is reported to have said that if faced with life as a 'vegetable', she would not want to live. She also said, among other things, that 'death is sometimes not the worst situation you can be in' when compared to being 'sent to the point of death and then stabilised' without any reasonable possibility of 'ever really getting better'. While Ms Cruzan could not have foreseen her accident, were her statements not the best guide to her own wishes?

The 1988 Cruzan opinion was more than a failure to hear and obey Nancy Cruzan's voice. It was a refusal to let her next-of-kin speak for her. This made a nonsense of the whole concept of surrogate decision-making about life-sustaining treatment for a patient who could no longer decide for herself. Historically, both legally and medically, the convention has been to turn to the patients' families, to let them act as their agents, deciding as they would to the best of their abilities. The Cruzan verdict rejected this, stating that if there was a right to refuse treatment it was based on the patient's own right to self-determination. The Cruzan verdict correctly stressed the gravity of a decision to forgo life-sustaining treatment. From that basis, the court concluded that this was not the sort of decision that can be ceded to a surrogate. However, the verdict fails to consider that the decision to continue treatment is also of the utmost gravity – because it condemned Nancy to potentially decades of invasive treatment in a vegetative state. This in turn raises the question of whether the best interests of patients, families and society are served by raising issues of terminating life-sustaining treatment in a constitutional forum?

A number of bills which would apparently legalise active killing have been introduced into various legislative bodies. As far back as 1936 a voluntary euthanasia bill was defeated in the UK's House of Lords. Many bills have also introduced to clarify the rights of competent patients. One of the seminal pieces of legislation in this respect was the Natural Death Act of California (1976). Its value was to make clear that instructions written while competent but after one is certifiably terminally ill remain valid, even when a patient lapses into incompetency.

However, the Act created more problems than it resolved. Firstly, it did not provide assurance that, if people wrote something while competent their wishes would be followed should they become terminally ill. It stated:

If the declarant becomes a qualified patient subsequent to executing the directive, and has not subsequently re-executed the directive, the attending physician may give weight (but)...may consider other factors such as information from the affected family or the nature of the patient's illness, injury or disease, in determining whether the totality of circumstances known to the attending physician justify effectuating the directive.

Specifically, it gives no assurance to anyone who fears being maintained after an accident or stroke. Secondly, the Act's definition of terminal illness is hopelessly inadequate. A terminal condition is described as an 'incurable condition caused by injury, disease, or illness which, regardless of the application of life-sustaining procedures, would, within reasonable medical judgement, produce death, and where the application of life-sustaining procedures serves only to postpone the moment of death of the patient'. This definition excludes many situations where treatment refusal is normally acceptable. Moreover, the directive takes effect only when death is 'imminent'. Accordingly, patients would be prevented from withdrawing treatment when they are declining and treatment has become burdensome and useless, but when death is still not imminent.

A FINE DISTINCTION

Many people, including those who are actively committed to right-to-life positions and to continued care for the terminally ill, are beginning to explore the legislative options to clarify the individual's right to control decisions about terminal care. This reflects a distaste of the excessive technologising process and its control by the professional rather than the family. One possible approach is to have no policy at all, to leave the practitioner to decide which treatments are or are not appropriate. Such an approach worked in the first half of this century, when technology was less advanced. Today there is such a proliferation of diverse views of what kind of care is appropriate that it would be impossible to get consistency. Another possible approach is for death to be authorised for a patient by giving the health-care professionals a wide discretion and trusting their sense of professional responsibility. Such a position carries too great a risk of abuse.

An absolute prohibition against euthanasia suggests that there are no limits to the obligation to sustain life. For this reason it is often argued that it is more helpful to conduct the debate in terms of putting to death and letting die. The goal of medicine is not to provide us with a way to live forever but to help us on the path to health. Accordingly, we need to recover a much more accepting attitude to death and a greater concern for the needs of the dying patient. To do this it is important to return to the practice of medicine the ethic of allowing a person to die. In ethical terms there is an onus on the person not to inflict life on another person in circumstances where that life would be painful and futile. One lawyer put it in the following way: 'Doctors are sometimes free – sometimes indeed required – to allow a patient to die.'

In ethical terms there is no essential distinction between killing and letting die – although in practical ethical terms, health-care professionals are ethically and legally justified in withholding or withdrawing any treatments that are not beneficial to their patients, and are ethically and legally required to withhold or withdraw any treatments that are harmful.

Let us illustrate with an example. A doctor is dealing with a chronically ill, debilitated patient with no known malignancy. While incompetent, this patient is not unconscious or in a persistent vegetative state. The physician in charge of the case concludes that aggressive therapy is not needed and that 'care and comfort' should be the treatment goal. The family agrees with this verdict and forcefully argues that the patient ought not be transferred to the hospital.

The problem arises with the doctor's interpretation of 'care and comfort'. Using supplemental oxygen, for example, was seen as part of basic care. However, when complications arise, the doctor prescribes antibiotics but the family objects, seeing it as an attempt to prolong the dying process. The doctor feels that it is not ethically acceptable to withhold potentially beneficial treatment from an incompetent patient – on the grounds that death is not imminent or life is not so burdensome for this patient that simple, inexpensive treatment should be denied. From this perspective, withholding the antibiotics crosses a fine line between *allowing* death and *causing* death.

Such cases, of course, raise a proliferation of difficult questions. What is a terminal illness when the demented patient can be kept going for years if nutrition is provided and infection treated? When is incompetence or ageing such a burden that any medical treatment, however simple and routine, is unnecessary and even undesirable? What do doctors owe to patients who cannot speak for themselves and who exist in a state they consider not worth living? How is a doctor to cope with incompetent patients if they never knew them when they were competent and have little knowledge of their families? What is the point of demarcation between routine and burdensome treatment?

The ideal is a patient who is calm, clear-headed and pain-free. Sadly, this is not always possible. As a rule of thumb, treatment should be geared to bring comfort to the patient – where comfort is a state of conscious physical and mental wellbeing. To speak of patient's choices in this area is unhelpful, because it obscures the distinction between request and refusal of treatment. This distinction is central to a discussion of questions of killing or letting die. Doctors are ethically and legally required to honour a competent patient's rational refusal of therapy. The moral and legal obligations do not stretch, however, to honouring a patient's request for specific therapy.

In the past Clough's rhyme has been used as a rule of thumb for doctors:

Thou shalt not kill; but
needs't not strive
officiously to keep alive.

This is said to offer a helpful guideline in the treatment
of terminally ill patients. For example if an elderly
patient with lung cancer, exhausted from continuous
coughing, got a chest infection a doctor would seriously
consider not treating it because it would only prolong a
patient's suffering – provided the infection was not
making the patient more distressed. In normal circumstances, with a patient not facing death, such an
infection would be treated vigorously with intravenous
antibiotics and a respirator. This highlights the danger of
making blanket rules about the treatment of terminally
ill patients.

The problem with Clough's rhyme is that it
perpetuates the notion of an alleged distinction
between killing and letting die. In ethical terms there is
no essential distinction between killing and letting die.
However, as Thomas Aquinas pointed out: 'Omission
means failing to do good, albeit not any good but only
the good that one ought to do.' An inaction is therefore
a morally inculpable inaction.

How actively we treat such terminally ill patients
will depend on their personal circumstances as well as
on their medical condition; for example, somebody
whose spouse is still living may wish for that reason to
cling on to a poor quality of life, whereas somebody
with a comparable medical condition who has no such
close relative may not wish to do so. Treatment should
always be provided to those who want it – and those
who will benefit from it. This second condition is an
important caveat because it is not ethically responsible

or acceptable for doctors to administer useless treatment – vainly trying to treat a person whose body has been so badly damaged that it can no longer sustain life.

THE RIGHT TO DIE

The vocabulary of rights is inappropriate to sound personal decision-making or to sensible public policy in this area. In light of the traumatic decisions that have to be taken, it is difficult enough for practical wisdom to try to discern what is the most responsible course of action to take, without the added burden of having to contend with intransigent and absolute demands of a legal or moral right to die. It is noteworthy that even some of its proponents tend to put 'right to die' in quotation marks, acknowledging this is at least a 'misnomer'. It is also interesting to observe that the former Euthanasia Society of America, shedding the Nazi-tainted and oft-criticised word 'euthanasia', changed its name to the Society for the Right to Die before becoming Choice In Dying.

The claim of a right to die is made only in Western countries – not surprisingly, since only in such societies do human beings look first to the rights of individuals and only there do we find the sophisticated health-care capable of keeping patients from dying when they might wish to do so. A right is a species of liberty. The seminal work on rights was formulated by Thomas Hobbes, who argued that a right was a blameless liberty. Not everything we are free to do, legally or ethically, do we have a right to do. Rights were claimed to defend the safety and dignity of the individual against the dominion of tyrant. However, in recent times, to add to the traditional, negative rights against interference with our liberties, efforts have been made to add certain so-called welfare rights – rights that give us certain entitlements, such as the right to a basic education. Despite this ever-expanding catalogue of rights, the sphere of rights is not unlimited; it is not possible to claim a right to wisdom, beauty or love.

The campaign for a right to die reflects an ever-growing aversion to the bio-medical project, which seeks, in principle, to prolong life indefinitely. It is the already available means to sustain life for a lengthy period of time, albeit not indefinitely, but much longer than is many cases reasonable or desirable, that has made death so untimely late as to appear a blessing. The phrase the 'right to die' is sometimes a code for the right to refuse such life-sustaining medical treatment. However, it normally embraces something more – not only how to live while dying but with a choice for death. In this sense the phrase 'the right to die' is not a misnomer. This is particularly the case of those who claim that the right to die encompasses the right to medically assisted suicide. In its most radical form, a right to die means a right to become or to be made dead, by whatever means. The ethics of treating the terminally ill must be based on the considerations of the welfare of the dying patients, rather than with reference to the benefits that might accrue to society or their families through their deaths.

PAST THE POINT OF RESCUE

Laws should make clear that wishes expressed while competent and never disavowed should remain valid when individuals are unable to express themselves. Procedures for disavowal must be clearly defined. If it is considered acceptable for a competent person to refuse medical treatment, even if it will lead to death, it is consistent to hold that the patient's wishes should remain valid when he or she is no longer competent. Penalties should also be specified for failure to follow such instructions. Equally, to protect the professionals involved, the law should make explicit that they are not guilty of homicide. Patients should be informed of the right to accept or refuse treatment.

The rights of health-care professionals should also be catered for. In particular the practitioner's professional conscience should be respected; a doctor should be free to withdraw from a case when the patient's instructions conflict with his or her ethical standpoint. Provision should also be made to provide adequate care from other practitioners for the patients in question. A minimum age – for example the age of majority – for execution of a treatment acceptance or refusal document should be stipulated. The law should also consider the problem of 'incompetent' patients.

In Washington, DC, in a very recent case, the doctors caring for baby Rena, an eighteen-month-old in constant pain with AIDS, hydrocephalus, respiratory distress, heart failure, and kidney dysfunction, believed that health care should not be used to torture the dying and made plans to go to court. Her foster parents insisted that all treatment must be continued, because God would definitely work a miracle. In these scenarios doctors do not want to be forced into providing treatment that they consider to be medically or ethically wrong. Families understandably do not want to be precluded from supporting the lives of their loved ones by the veto of doctors who have monopoly control over the means to those patients' survival.

Another party to be considered is the taxpayer, who

pays the taxes and insurance premiums that fund such care and who may be concerned where they see 'social hijacking' committed by patients and families pursuing private goals at common expense.

The Warnock Report on Human Fertilisation and Embryology represents a concerted attempt to define the moral role in liberal terms – attempting to legislate on the basis of a perceived implicit consensus. However, the Wolfenden report on homosexuality and the Williams Report on pornography both abandoned the effort to establish a substantive consensus, opting for a course that made a distinction between two realms – in other words a public realm where ethics is enforced by a law, and a private sphere within which individuals are left free to act on their own ethical preferences. A key function of a law is to protect the most vulnerable sections of the community, for example the severely disabled and the terminally ill, who might be threatened by prejudice. In Japan, for example, in 1987 there was a fundamental revision of legal procedures of the medical care and custody of mentally disordered people. This was a long overdue corrective to the 1950 Mental Health Law, which was enacted with the intent to protect society from the sinisterly termed 'harmful insane people' – which effectively deprived these people of their fundamental human rights.

Particular legal problems arise in the treatment of terminally ill patients who are no longer competent.

GUIDELINES
When a patient is unable to make a competent decision because of sedation, it may be possible to reduce the sedation for a brief period to allow for a lucid decision to be made. Although the ideal is to ask the patient

their views of treatment, there are four situations when this is particularly problematic:

- the terminally ill patient who is sedated because of severe distress and or pain;
- cases of 'terminal agitated delirium', i.e. the terminally ill patient who is also mentally ill and who is sedated because of increased agitation;
- disagreement about the appropriate management between, on the one hand, the medical and nursing staff, and on the other hand, close members of the patient's family;
- family members who themselves have medical expertise disagree with the medical carers.

In these circumstances it is difficult to achieve consensus.

What does 'consensus' mean? According to dictionary definitions the word means 'agreement', 'concord of opinion', 'common view' or 'common understanding'. Consensus has become a buzz-word in contemporary health-care and implies agreement. However, agreement in the medical context is often agreement in spite of disagreement, because of different opinions of treatment choices. There are a number of guidelines to refer to in such situations, notably the Appleton International Consensus and the British Medical Association (BMA) guidelines. The BMA states that, when deciding whether life-prolonging treatment is in the best interests of the patient, the health-care team should consider three main factors:

1. the possibility of extending life under humane and comfortable conditions;

2. the patient's values about life and the way it should be lived;
3. the patient's likely reaction to sickness, suffering and medical intervention.

The BMA also points out:
> Although doctors should not give treatment simply because it is available, in cases of doubt about the best interest of the patient, the presumption should be in favour of prolonging life. This is particularly so if most people would consider that life to be of acceptable quality.

The guidelines go on to state that in cases of disagreement between doctors and patients' proxies time and effort should be put into 'counselling, discussion and further medical opinion' and recommend that as far as possible such conflicts should be resolved without recourse to the courts. However, should disagreement remain, the doctor should not, except in the most exceptional circumstances, override the proxies position without resorting to more formal conflict-resolution mechanisms.

Who should have guardianship when a patient is no longer competent? The natural choice would be someone the patient has designated while competent. The situation is much more problematic when nobody has been designated by the patient while competent. In normal circumstances the next-of-kin would be appointed. Laws promulgated in this area must serve two functions:

- to nurture patient and familial integrity and self-determination. However, problems arise when family

members disagree about the course of treatment.;
- to explicate the proper decision-making authority, i.e. to clarify which decisions are legally binding and who has the authority to make such judgements.

It may be that a court of law is not the best forum to resolve this issue, because of a lack of specific medical expertise. Perhaps the creation of some kind of national mediation service comprising legal and medical expertise and patients' representatives could be piloted. For the sake of the reputation of medicine it is important that not only should justice be done, it should be seen to be done.

Ethics consultations, requested to help sort out what are deemed to be ethical problems in patient care, are becoming more prevalent. Conflicts may arise not only between doctors and patients but also among members of the health-care team when it comes to formulating and choosing goals of treatment. Such conflicts most commonly occur when:

1. patients and doctors disagree on goals;
2. doctors and patients agree on the goals but the means necessary to procure such goals are ethically not acceptable to one of the parties;
3. doctors, family and members of the health-care team have different goals in view;
4. no clear goals have been decided upon;
5. the patient is incompetent, the patient has expressed no prior wishes in regard to the goals of treatment, and no clearly acceptable surrogates are known.

Ethics committees serve three valuable functions:

1. Helping to furnish options and formulating choices
2. Bringing all interested parties in a dialogue
3. Decreasing the frequent feelings of powerlessness and guilt which all concerned have when dealing with issues in which no ideal solution is available.

Ethics committees cannot resolve every conflict, because ethics is ultimately a matter for individual agents and because the key question remains 'What am I supposed to do?' A particular focus of such arbitration procedures is to ensure that the best interests of the patient should not take second place to the emotional distress of the relatives.

Seven

Sliding Down the Slippery Slope?

Across western society the growing cultural diversity of patients and health care professionals has multiplied the obstacles to clinical consensus. Since the 1973 Leeuwarden trial of a doctor who killed a patient requesting euthanasia, public debate on euthanasia in Holland has been very wide-ranging. Early in 1989 two legislative proposals dealing with euthanasia were submitted to parliament but in fact were never debated, as shortly afterwards the cabinet resigned. That November the coalition government, of the Christian Democratic Party and the Socialist Party, decided to suspend political debate on legislation in order that they might get comprehensive statistical data of the frequency and nature of euthanasia in medical practice. In January 1990 a new committee comprising of three doctors and three lawyers was established by the Ministers of Justice and Public Health to examine medical practices connected with the end of life. In September 1991 the committee published its report, followed by new legislative proposals issued by the government on 8 November 1991 with the proviso for a discussion in parliament the following May. In December 1990 a two-day international conference held in Maastricht, made up of seven Dutch and seven international experts, examined the practice of euthanasia in the Netherlands.

The significance of these developments is that they shift the debate from the realm of bioethics, that is, assessing the merits or otherwise of euthanasia within the doctor–patient relationship, to the wider socio-political context of whether and how to regulate or legalise the actual practice of euthanasia, given newly accumulated empirical data. Medical–ethical viewpoints regarding euthanasia in the clinical setting have in some respects faded to the background.

The definition of euthanasia widely accepted in Netherlands is: the active termination of a patient's life at his or her request by a doctor. Contrary to popular perception, euthanasia is specifically prohibited by Article 293 of the Dutch Penal Code: 'He who takes the life of another person on this person's explicit and serious request will be punished with imprisonment of up to twelve years or a fine of the Fifth Category [as much as 60 thousand US dollars].' Moreover, it is not true to say that euthanasia is accepted in the Netherlands. Although debate and practice are more open in the Netherlands than in other western countries, Dutch society recognises that many problematic questions linger.

In practice, physicians who adhere to three crucial conditions recognised by the courts and endorsed by the State Commission on Euthanasia in 1985 are in practice not subject to criminal sanctions:

1. **voluntariness** – the patient's request must be persistent, conscious, and freely made. In Holland

'voluntary euthanasia' is a tautology and 'involuntary euthanasia' a contradiction in terms;

2. **unbearable suffering** – the patient's suffering, including but not limited to physical pain, cannot be relieved by any other means. Both patient and physician must consider the patient's condition to be beyond recovery or improvement;

3. **consultation** – the attending doctor must consult with a colleague regarding the patient's condition and the authenticity and appropriateness of the request for euthanasia.

Dutch law specifies that physicians are obliged accurately to report the cause of death. While this measure is not explicitly directed toward the practice of euthanasia it does act, at least nominally, as an in-built safety mechanism.

DEATH AFTER A COMA

The euthanasia debate in the Netherlands was fuelled further when Mrs Ineke Stinissen died in January 1990 after having been in a coma for fifteen years following an anaesthetic accident which occurred in the course of a Caesarean section operation. During her comatose years she had been hydrated and fed through nasogastric tube. Her death followed shortly after the courts declared that her feeding and hydration constituted medical treatment, whereupon the practitioners discontinued her treatment. The case provoked a massive controversy throughout the length and breath of Holland on the ethics of treatment decisions for comatose patients. The shape of the debate was to a large extent determined by a much wider conflict in public opinion on active euthanasia.

Since the early 1970s a convention has emerged in the Dutch health-care system in which euthanatising patients is not judicially prosecuted as long as particular procedural conditions have been fulfilled. This approach took its lead from the emergence of the concept of the 'persistent vegetative state' in the 1970s – a concept which relieved doctors of the obligation to provide artificial administration of food and fluid when treatment was considered to be useless. The key condition is the explicit, repeatedly expressed wish of the patient. Some commentators fear that the controversy on comatose patients jeopardises the fickle consensus in relation to this practice. On the other hand, some see it as part of a concerted effort to eliminate the unproductive members of society. Is there a quality-of-life judgement involved in such a clinical judgement? What is the ethical status of PVS patients? Can they be said to be in the process of dying or not? Ought they be considered dead? Is there biological or personal existence? Who should make judgements in the case of incompetent patients?

THE LAW AT ARM'S LENGTH

Also in 1990 the Minister of Justice instructed prosecutors that they were no longer to request the police to investigate euthanasia cases unless there was some reason to suspect that there had not been compliance with the criteria. The directive was issued despite the advice of chief prosecutors on the grounds that it caused them to lower their professional standards below the absolute minimum, and that the examination conducted by the medical examiner was simply a chat between colleagues and not an inquiry at all. This instruction was welcomed by health-care professionals, who viewed it as an expression of the minister's agreement that decisions about euthanasia should be taken by the medical profession rather than the legal profession. Doctors tend to be opposed to the idea of reporting euthanasia – in order to spare the deceased's relatives a police inquiry. A number of studies have uncovered disturbing evidence about the practice of euthanasia in Holland.

THE DOCTOR'S DILEMMA

PJ van der Maas *et al.*'s *Euthanasia and other medical decisions concerning the end of life* (1992) is an important study, if for no other reason than that it is a measured effort to temper some of the wilder claims and counter-claims about the practices of euthanasia in the Netherlands. The book is based on interviews with over 400 Dutch doctors who also collaborated in a study and on data related to a sample of approximately 8,500 death certificates.

It discovered that in 1990, 2,300 or 1.8 per cent of all deaths could be classified as euthanasia understood as 'purposeful acting to terminate life by someone other than the person concerned upon the request of the latter' and 400 or 0.35 per cent as assisted suicide. The lives of 1,000 patients (0.8 per cent of all deaths) were terminated without explicit request; and in the case of 22,500 others (17.5 per cent of all deaths) pain was reduced by taking treatment which could shorten life. Very few patients in any of these groups were likely to have survived for longer than six months, and many had only days or hours to live. Almost all significant shortening of life was in the further category of decisions to withhold or withdraw treatment, which would prolong by disproportionate means.

Not surprisingly the initial reaction to the study zoomed in on the figure of one thousand 'life-terminating acts without request'. The book suggests that over half of the patients involved had indicated at a previous juncture that they would have wanted their lives ended in those circumstances. Almost all of those whose wishes were not known were terminally ill, suffering seriously, or no longer able to make their intentions known.

The study found that 62 per cent of Dutch doctors had performed euthanasia at some time, but also that two thirds of requests were not acceded to. Such a high percentage of refusals does not nestle comfortably with the stereotype of frail, elderly people being pressurised by enthusiastic doctors. One positive feature which emerged from the study was the apparent willingness of Dutch doctors to have their decisions scrutinised by outsiders.

One of the problems about interpreting this study is that medical judgements about the terminating of life are more nuanced than reflected in the definition. Many doctors do not interpret or classify their actions as euthanasia, even when those actions fall under the range of the definition employed in the report. For this reason the figure of 2,300 is not a reliable indicator of medical decisions leading to patients' death. However, the report indicates that other forms of intentional hastening of death are widespread in Holland but escape professional, judicial and social scrutiny. A different complexion emerges if we consider that in 6 per cent of the total number of 22,500 cases in which pain medication with a possible lethal effect was administered, hastening death was the main objective of the administration, and it was at least one of the objectives in almost 30 per cent of the cases. To include these figures would increase the incidence of euthanasia to 8,100 cases.

One of the curious features about the study is that in 28 per cent of these 1,000 cases, patients had previously expressed their wish for euthanasia if, for example, the pain ever became unbearable or their situation inhuman. However, doctors referred to 'previously uttered request of the patient' as their reason for euthanasia in only 17 per cent of the cases. The authors claim that this discrepancy can be explained by arguing that doctors tend to be directed by their own impressions of the patient's unspoken but probable wishes than by explicit oral or written requests – this despite the fact that many courts have ruled that suffering is purely subjective, i.e. only patients themselves can decide whether or not their suffering has become unbearable. Are such 'impressions' justified? There is an apparent split phenomenon in attitudes to euthanasia in Holland. Advocates employ the subjective argument when defending the right of the competent patient to opt for euthanasia autonomously, and the impressionist argument when defending the practice of euthanasia on the mentally incompetent patient.

A study also found that in 45 per cent of the 1,000 involuntary euthanasia cases, treatment of pain was no longer adequate to relieve the patient's suffering. However, the inability to treat pain satisfactorily was the reason for killing the patient in only 30 per cent of the cases. The remaining 70 per cent were killed for a variety of reasons, for example low quality of life, no prospect of improvement, the futility of treatment, the patient did not die even though treatment was withdrawn or one should not postpone death. In over 30 per cent of the cases, the fact that family and friends no longer could bear the situation played a role in the decision-making. One of the respondents suggested that economic considerations, such as shortage of beds, played a role. These findings indicate that the three criteria we have considered are not the only circumstances in which euthanasia is practised.

SITTING IN JUDGEMENT

The results of a survey of general practitioners carried out by Gerrit van der Wal, himself a medical examiner, published in 1991 revealed disturbing findings. It showed that the interval between the first request for euthanasia and its performance was no more than a day in 13 per cent of cases; no more than a week in another 35 per cent; and between a week and a fortnight in a further 17 per cent. Moreover, the gap between the last request for euthanasia and its performance was, in three out of five cases, no more than a day. In 22 per cent of cases there was, in a clear breach of the guidelines, only a single request and in a further 30 per cent of cases the interval between the first and last requests was between an hour and a week. In addition, in approximately 60 per cent of cases the request was simply spoken.

The survey's results in relation to consultation offer further disquieting evidence: 'One quarter of the general practitioners said they had not had *consultation* prior to euthanasia/assisted suicide...More serious is the finding that 12 per cent...manifestly had no form of *discussion* with any other caregivers...a substantial proportion of general practitioners is not (yet) operating in accordance with current procedural precautionary requirements.' When consultation did occur, the second opinion was in most cases a colleague rather than an independent practitioner; the second physician already knew the patient in about two thirds of cases.

FOOD FOR THOUGHT
Carlos F. Gomez, in an effort to reach an accurate understanding of the reality of euthanasia in the Netherlands in January 1989, carried out structured interviews with nine separate sources of information: one terminal-care team, five doctors, one nurse, a relative of a euthanised patient, and an ethicist consulted in euthanasia cases. Employing a set of ten criteria, vetted by some of the foremost Dutch experts to ensure that they accurately reflected the consensus on permissible euthanasia, Gomez requested the interviewees to describe cases of euthanasia in which they had an involvement over the previous five years. Having considered their responses, Gomez remarked: 'it seems clear...that the guidelines put forth are being variously interpreted, and in some cases, they are ignored altogether.' Such cases offered conclusive evidence of an expansive interpretation of 'unbearable suffering' and 'last resort' and indicated both how the determination of voluntariness resided with physicians and the way in which standards for making this determination varied considerably. In addition although physicians ought to have made the case available for investigation by the prosecutor, in fewer than 2 per cent of cases was the prosecutor notified.

Gomez went on to claim that 'the formal, juridical level' of the regulatory mechanism is 'routinely bypassed'; that the informal regulatory procedures are poorly policed and, because of the lack of clarity, unpolicable; and that the Dutch system is prompted chiefly by private discretion rather than by public control. He reserves his strongest language for the medical profession's failure to protect the most vulnerable section of Dutch society because of their 'almost cavalier attitude toward those – however many or few their numbers – who cannot challenge a decision to have euthanasia performed upon them.' He goes on to underscore his criticism of Dutch public policy for creating a 'private place' for euthanasia because of a widespread failure of practitioners to notify the authorities and, second, even when the authorities have been notified, by an unwillingness of the prosecutors to prosecute and of courts to convict. This reticence stems from the fact that it is the physicians who determine what is reported and they are unlikely to include anything incriminatory. In a remarkable piece of under-statement he describes the loose regulatory procedures as 'less than reassuring'. He contends that on the 'core issues' of the euthanasia controversy, i.e. 'how to control the practice, how to keep it from being used on those who do not want it, how to provide for account-ability', the Dutch response is 'inadequate'. The narrator of John Updike's novel *Couples* suggests after Foxy's abortion: 'Death, once invited in, leaves his muddy bloodprints everywhere.' To accept a lax policy of policing on euthanasia is to slide on the slippery slope.

WEIGHING THE EVIDENCE
The Dutch system has its merits. Firstly, it is a serious attempt to confront a deep ambivalence that many people have about euthanasia arising from a strong commitment to the value of self-determination on the one hand and a deep reverence for life on the other.

Secondly, it is a recognition of the need to consider the particularities, the complexities and ambiguities of the human context in which we must make individualised choices about life and death. Thirdly, it avoids using the language of rights – a language which, as we have seen, is an unhelpful way of approaching the issue. To speak of the 'right to die' is a very odd way to talk of a natural inevitability! Fourthly, it explicitly recognises that prolonging futile treatment is unnecessary – though its understanding of futility is at best questionable.

However, the disadvantages significantly outweigh the advantages. Firstly, if we accept that euthanasia is a legitimate exercise of the autonomy of the patient how could a health-care professional ever refuse a request for euthanasia? Secondly, even if we accept the dubious proposition that the patient has a right to self-determination even unto death, how is this right transferable to another, i.e. a proxy? Thirdly, since suffering is in principle and forever unverifiable and has no objective correlation with a patient's medical condition, how could a doctor ever be sure that a patient's suffering was genuinely unbearable? Fourthly, the requirement for consultation seems to be little more than a sham when concurring opinions can be sought from physicians well known to be sympathetic to the practice of euthanasia. Fifthly, it is difficult to have much confidence in the system of regulation with the apparently totally inadequate investigation into under-reporting. Sixthly, the guidelines seemingly ignore that to kill a patient at that patient's request is a radical departure from the longstanding Hippocratic tradition of medical consciousness. Does the Dutch policy not fundamentally conflict with the very essence of medical practice? The duty of the doctor to relieve suffering does not encompass killing the patient in order to end the suffering. It is not the task of medicine to erase suffering altogether. While human beings have the right to aim at managing their own destinies or to avoid unnecessary suffering we have to accept that death eventually escapes our control. In this respect the guidelines can be said to perpetuate the ideology of control, the goal of mastering life and death. Seventhly, the guidelines give too much power to the medical profession. It is effectively gifted with the power to directly and deliberately take life.

The 'voluntariness' provision merits particular scrutiny because it suggests that euthanasia might be an extension of the right to self-determination. However, euthanasia cannot be limited in this way, because it requires the doctor to act and involves the regulation and oversight of the government. Euthanasia can never be the patient's individual decision, since the doctor must agree that the patient's life, being a life of suffering, is not worth living.

CONCLUSION

Since the 1970s euthanasia has been a widely discussed issue in Holland. It began as a protest against the power of contemporary health care to alienate individuals from their own dying. Instead of counterbalancing that power and enhancing personal autonomy it appears that social acceptance of euthanasia has resulted in physicians' acquiring even more control over the life and death of patients. Studies indicate that in most cases of terminating human life, it is, in fact, the doctors who decide that it is appropriate to hasten death; the patient's voluntary and persistent request is often casually brushed aside. In addition these studies have shown that euthanasia is being practised on a scale vastly exceeding the number of truthfully reported and recorded cases.

The word 'trust' is sometimes used in an ironic way, for example Joseph Heller's character Slocum in *Something Happened!* describes a character: 'He knows I drink and lie and whore around a lot, and he therefore feels that he can trust me.' However, in relation to health care trust includes the expectation that doctors will respect certain ethical limits. This appears not always to be the case in Holland as the so-called control mechanisms against indiscriminate euthanasia are ineffectual. It appears the solution has become the problem.

Eight

To Will or Not to Will?

Advance directives, such as living wills, durable powers of attorney, appointment of health-care proxies and other procedures that allow competent people to give directions concerning their medical treatment, have become commonplace. In the United States, for example, they have achieved judicial or legislative recognition in many states. Their popularity can be attributed to two factors. Firstly, they give competent people a feeling of control should they become incompetent at a future point. In this way advance directives empower people, by continuing the scope of personal self-determination to circumstances in which autonomy cannot be directly exercised. People, when competent, determine the course of their lives when incompetent, thereby ensuring that they will be treated with reference to their previously stated wishes.

Secondly, advance directives take away the fear that at some time in the future people will be forced to endure treatment which leaves them with little or no dignity. They are said to provide a framework for non-treatment decisions which respect autonomy without jeopardising respect for incompetent patients. Moreover, they stipulate that treatment can be withheld, in certain circumstances, from both incompetent and competent patients.

In the light of these advantages, advance directives clearly have an appeal. Perhaps the most fruitful avenue to explore their merits and demerits is to evaluate their effectiveness in two countries where they have become popular.

THE GREAT DANISH DEBATE

In 1992 the Danish parliament passed a law in relation to advance directives (L 1992-05-14 no. 351). This new measure stipulated a standardised format and created a central national register for advance directives. Up until then, all a doctor had for guidance was a press release from the Danish Board of Health, going back to 1974, which simply stated that it was compatible with Danish law to discontinue futile treatment. A vigorous lobbying campaign by a group called 'My Living Will' had sought the legal recognition of advance directives since 1976. Advance directives are registered only if they are presented on the appropriate form. No witnesses are required, but the registrar is obliged to write back to the individual in question and request a small registration fee to ensure that the individual whose address and personal ID number are on the form was the person who actually filled it in. The form has three sections, which outline the following separate scenarios:

1. I do not want life-extending treatment if I am in a situation where I am irreversibly dying.
2. I do not want life-extending treatment in cases where

disease, advanced senility, accident, cardiac arrest, or similar conditions have caused such a severe state of disability that I will be permanently physically and mentally unable to take care of myself.

3. If the situation described in part one should occur I do want to be kept free from pain with pain-relieving/sedative drugs, even though this may hasten the moment of death.

The law stipulates that the wish expressed in the first section must never be violated, though the wishes expressed in the other two sections can be overridden, but only after assiduous reflection on the part of the doctor in charge. Such a directive becomes active the moment the condition described in part one or two obtains, and Danish physicians are required to phone the register whenever they begin treating a patient in one of these situations. Only forty such calls had been made six months after the register was established. This reflected to some extent the hostility of the Danish Medical Association to this piece of legislation because of a combination of factors. Firstly, there is no time limit on the validity of an advance directive. Secondly, in view of the comparative ease and informality of registering an advance directive, there is no way of ensuring that the individual in question is competent to make such a decision. Thirdly, some of the phrasing is very ambiguous, e.g. 'I am irreversibly dying' and 'that I will be permanently physically and mentally unable to take care of myself' lend themselves to different interpretations. Fourthly, the procedure to establish if an advance directive is registered takes inadequate consideration of the reality of medical practice, i.e. expecting an emergency-room doctor to leave a patient just to phone the register and wait until the call is returned.

One year after the register was established, 65,000 registered advance directives, out of an adult population of 3.9 million, had been effected. Interestingly, two-thirds of these were registered by women. By comparison with the comparable legislation in the US, the Danish system has two advantages and one disadvantage. Positively, the system is simple and the central register allows for an easy check to establish if a directive has been registered. On the down side, the choice is very limited. What then of the system in the US?

OF THE PATIENT, FOR THE PATIENT, BY THE PATIENT

The most important piece of legislation in this area was the Patient Self-Determination Act (PSDA) which became law in December 1991. It was designed to 'enhance an individual's control over medical treatment decisions' by championing the cause of advance directives. Apart from stipulating that health-care providers inform competent adult patients of the possibility of executing directives, the Act deliberately gave providers little in the way of instructions. The following March the Health-Care Financing Administration published its 'interim final rule' which provided great latitude to institutions in fulfilling the federal mandate. Accordingly, particular institutions may attempt to implement the Act's requirements in their own way, for example in the way they inform patients about directives or document the directives in their medical records. The law could be summed up in the phrase: 'Thou shalt inform, ask, and educate.'

Practitioners reacted to this law in a contradictory way. On the one hand they insisted that flexibility is an essential prerequisite to nurturing genuine patient autonomy. On the other hand they have called for more specifics, that is in relation to who should receive information about health-care decision-making rights, when they must receive it, how and when to document advance directives, and how providers can or cannot follow their consciences in complying with patient directives. The interim rule requests that carers would establish the existence or otherwise of a directive at the beginning – by asking patients at admission if they have an advance directive. Carers must 'document in the individual's medical record whether or not the individual has executed an advance directive'.

One issue to be resolved is whether or not to require face-to-face dialogue with patients rather than simply relying written questionnaires in admission or preadmission materials to establish the existence of an advance directive. Patient groups tend to stress the importance of face-to-face dialogue, but provider groups tend to be more divided. Direct dialogue is very time consuming, but it offers a more helpful starting point since it provides a better opportunity for ensuring understanding, accuracy, and referral when individuals or family members require additional information.

A second question arises about access to the document itself: is it essential for a copy to be entered into the records? If a patient simply indicates that one exists, how much energy ought the provider expend in confirming the actual existence of the document? Studies indicate that providers tend to leave the burden of responsibility on the patients in this area. Currently providers are only obliged to 'document the directive'. They are not explicitly required to put a directive in the medical record, even if the patient hands a copy to the provider. Most advance-directive laws stipulate that providers must place a copy in the medical record.

THE CONSCIENTIOUS OBJECTOR

The PSDA states that carers are free not to implement advance directives based on conscience if state law allows such objections. However, every adult patient must be given written information about the institution's practices in order that potential conscience objections will be known in advance. The interim rule goes a step further and stipulates that carers give a 'clear and precise statement of limitation of services based on conscience'.

This leaves one unanswered question: how much information must carers impart about their policies, especially if facility policy defers to individual health-care professionals? As a norm carers argue that the 'clear and precise' standard is unrealistic, because institutions cannot possibly unravel and convey to patients the particular views of individual staff, particularly as it is the doctors' obligations to impart such information to patients. Moreover, many providers tend to use general and flexible principles, so objections are rarely categorical. They occur on a case-by-case basis.

Patient advocacy groups tend to adopt a contrary position, claiming that the 'clear and precise' standard is inadequate. Conscientious objections can be raised as a device to avoid compliance with patient preferences. Accordingly, some groups are lobbying for the elements of a clear and precise explanation to be spelled out, to include an explanation of steps to be taken if the carer fails to comply at the moment a decision needs to be taken. Without making such elements explicit, 'clear and precise' rests solely in the eyes of the beholder.

In response to this debate the American Bar Association Commission on Legal Problems of the Elderly suggest that provider policies ought:

1. clarify any differences between institution-wide conscience objections and those that could be raised by individual doctors;
2. explain the basis for any institutional objection, e.g. religious ethos;
3. name the state authority permitting such objection;
4. outline the range of medical conditions or procedures affected by conscience objections;
5. identify what measures will be taken to cater for patients whose desires are impeded by the institution's policy.

Such guidelines are not meant to restrict objections based on conscience, but to guarantee that patients' directives will contain common, identifiable key elements.

GREAT EXPECTATIONS

The PSDA was intended to usher in a new era in which patient autonomy would be enhanced. However, this is to assume that advance directives automatically serve the patient's interests. It might be argued that they could be expensive, meaningless or harmful. If that were the case encouraging their use would not be ethically responsible.

Advance directives are favoured by many, since they are said to enable decisions made in the treatment of a patient to deliver the optimum outcome for the patient, as perceived by the patient. Since long-term illness is frequently the by-product of old age, doctors can anticipate incompetence and enable patients to direct in advance the kinds of care they would aspire to. This protects the patient's *almost absolute* authority at a time of incompetence and consequently simplifies decision-making, by making it quicker and more in keeping with the patient's own preferences. Having the patient make decisions in advance of incompetence allows others to avoid the often difficult and uncertain task of making the choices and allows the patient to continue to have responsibility for decisions. 'Living wills' and 'durable powers of attorney' are the most common formal measures used to implement this objective. While the theory sounds compelling is the practice effective?

In the US most people have some familiarity with the concept of 'living wills' in particular, and advance directives in general. AIDS support groups have been particularly successful in ensuring their members are well informed on this topic. Studies suggest that while advance directives enjoy widespread approval, the rate at which they are actually written is much lower and varies with the population. In 1988 an opinion poll commissioned by the American Medical Association found that 56 per cent of the general population had discussed with family their preferences if they were in a coma - yet only 15 per cent had a living will. A subsequent study found that over 90 per cent of respondents had a positive attitude toward advance directives but less than 10 per cent had completed one. Significantly approximately 20 per cent of AIDS patients have written directives. A study carried out by SUPPORT (The Study to Understand Prognoses and Preferences for Outcomes and Risks of Treatments) established that 21 per cent of a population of very seriously ill hospitalised patients have advance directives, with 7 per cent living wills only, 9 per cent durable powers of attorney only and 5 per cent having both.

Characteristics associated with completing living wills are known only for particular populations with limited generalisability, e.g. AIDS patients and white or well-educated people are more likely to have written a directive. In one study 91 per cent of whites and 66 per cent of blacks expressed an intent to complete an advance directive. A recurring fear in relation to advance directives is that their meaning and usefulness might be linked to a rational 'middle class' approach to health care. What value has an advanced directive for someone who cannot afford health care? There have been few pilot studies to establish whether the rate of advance directive use can be improved which makes it difficult to establish the potential for increasing the rate of use.

LET THE SIGNER BEWARE

From what we have seen, it appears that the issue of advance directives has not formed a central part of the doctor–patient consultation. In the study of the AIDS population which we have already mentioned, only one-half of persons with an advance directive discussed it with a doctor, even after surviving a year of treatment. A SUPPORT study found that of 735 patients who were reported, either by self or surrogate, to have an advance directive, its existence was referred to in the doctor or nurse progress notes in only 45 cases. This study associates patient/surrogate preferences against resuscitation with having a living will. This indicates that patients may intend more to avoid loss of control while dying and incompetent, than to shape a palliative plan of care throughout the course of their terminal illness.

As advance directives tend to be vague and difficult to interpret, it is important to establish what the patient understood they were signing on for, and what he or she was seeking to achieve by completing the directive. To date, though, no studies have surveyed patients to establish what they were doing and how confident they were that they had succeeded. Similarly, no study has investigated the motivation for these directives, for example fear of loss of control or a concern for the wellbeing of one's family.

On the surface advance directives might serve one positive purpose – keeping decision-making out of the courts. The reality is otherwise. In fact, the opportunities for legal wrangling may escalate rather than decline, since the wordings are often too vague for ready application or are clouded by uncertainty about patient understanding at the time the directive was formulated.

A plethora of research projects has established that surrogates (normally next of kin) err significantly in predicting patient preferences. This is sometimes taken as a compelling argument for encouraging advance directives, since referral to family members appears unreliable. However, there is evidence that patients who do make living wills are more concerned with who makes the choices than which choices are made.

A particular concern is whether or not preferences expressed during a period of health and in advance of an urgent need for a decision endure into a time of serious illness. The limited studies which have already been carried out note that a significant number of people change their stated preferences. Thus a question arises as to the status of living wills when competent patients disagree later with what they said earlier in a formal advance directive.

Advance directives serve a useful function when they improve decision-making. Detailed interviews with 57 doctors from California and Vermont offer little to suggest that advance directives were useful in medical decision-making. Another study conducted by a group of doctors discovered that one in four directives was not honoured by the attending doctors. What is not clear is the reason for these failures and whether these breaches of directives were justified or not. Involving doctors at an early stage is essential if advance directives are to achieve the desired results. Ideally, doctors should meet patients when they are competent and learn about their wishes, values and fears. They would discuss long-range treatment possibilities, elicit preferences for care under various circumstances, and formulate medical goals consistent with their personal philosophies and beliefs. In this way they would be essentially patient advocates rather than primarily advocates for particular forms of treatment. Consequently they would get a sense of what particular patients would prefer in various circumstances. They would encourage people to name an agent who would be their spokesperson.

Only a handful of studies have addressed the key question of whether treatment differs between patients with and without living wills. One study from the SUPPORT group suggests that very sick people with and without advance directives by and large get the same care patterns even if the advance directives specify treatments. Living wills offer no help in distinguishing those situations of incompetent existence that have value for incompetent patients.

A FOG OF CONFUSION

Perhaps the central problem with advance directives is that the assumptions underlying their use are ambiguous or not clearly distinguished. The popular perception is that giving competent people control over decisions when they are incompetent patients safeguards their interests, because they are best placed to determine what their future interest will be. Accordingly, an advance directive is seen as the most accurate indicator of patients' interests once they become incompetent.

The difficulty is that a patient's interests when incompetent differ radically from when they were competent. The values and interests of the competent person are no longer relevant to someone who has lost the rational structure on which these values and interests are informed. It might be assumed that because previously competent persons have a history of values and preferences, they should be treated as having the same values and interests even when they become incompetent. However, this is to overlook the fact that at different stages and times of life we have different interests. When our circumstances alter dramatically, our interests and preferences also change. The difference between competent and incompetent interests is so great that if we are to respect incompetent interests, we are obliged to cater for their concerns in the here-and-now rather than retaining preferences which, as a result of their incompetency, no longer apply.

There is a very real danger that advance directives

could pose a serious risk to a patient's welfare when competent and incompetent interests diverge. Such directives, which reflect competent values and interests, may not accurately reflect the interests of an incompetent patient in the new situation – where values and interests dependent on a rational structure no longer pertain. The predicament of the incompetent patient is initially perceived through the eyes of the competent person rather than when they are incompetent – which undermines the more limited interests of a patient no longer animated by the concerns that motivated them when they were competent.

The need of the competent person for control and certainty, and the need of the incompetent patient for treatment, do not necessarily coincide. The competent person's advance certainty is bought at the possible cost of denying treatment to the incompetent person he or she has become. To date there have been no conclusive studies about the frequency of which incompetent interests have interests in being treated that are denied on the basis of advance directives. However, there is much anecdotal evidence to suggest that many patients who are treated despite a directive make a full recovery and are grateful. As advance directives become more widespread, such conflicts will increase. In many cases of terminal illness there is no conflict, because the incompetent patient will have no current interest in treatment. Advance directives, though, should not be needed to have such treatment withheld.

For this reason, doubts arise about whether those who execute living wills are exercising autonomy in an informed way if they are not even conscious of the conflict. Seldom are they told that their directives reflect their current interests and may not be a good indicator of their interest as an incompetent patient. In the absence of such information advance directives may not be made in an informed manner. The central issue is whether treatment or nontreatment best serves the interests of the now incompetent patient. Since the patient is effectively inhabiting a new world, advance directives may not be the most effective tool to deliver this outcome. One way forward would be for mandatory instruction of the potential conflict between their future interests when incompetent and their current interest in achieving certainty about how they will be treated to the makers of advance directives.

Yet a further complication is that if living wills and advance directives in general are to control even when patient interests conflict, would not this same principle apply to other directives that regulate the future, for instance surrogate mother contracts? Autonomy in controlling the future by prior directives is the distinguishing characteristic in both cases.

It is also important to consider the type of advance directive. While many are helpful, others may be unreasonably expensive or misleading. It is difficult to define the necessary components of a formal advance directive. Is it essential to meet the statutory requirements in relation to registration and witnessing? Is it mandatory to involve some doctor in the process? In the case of an instruction directive, is it sufficient to articulate broad principles about the appropriateness of dying, or must it also refer to more specific issues, for example the acceptance of particular treatments or outcomes? Should a directive have any weight if it is the fruit of a grave misunderstanding on the part of patients about their situations and their likely outcomes? More fundamentally, is a written document ever as important as comprehensive oral communication about preferences and likely outcomes betwee patient, providers, and potential surrogates? There is also the complication of informal advance directives, e.g. oral communications, letters, medical records ecetera. They are more difficult to measure and very few studies have been carried out about their efficiacy. However, such informal directives tend to be more helpful in the clinical setting than formal advance directives.

In an article in *The Hastings Center Report* (January–February 1993) Joanne Lynn and Joan M. Teno identify the crucial issue about the merits of living wills and advance directives:

> Making decisions in advance of incompetence seems to reconstitute the competent decision-maker and to evade the obvious ambiguities and compromises inherent in allowing decisions to be made by physicians and families. What is not clear is that the solution works or, more precisely, that it works better than alternative strategies. Nor is it clear that we have a common conception of what it would mean to 'work'; that is, what is the standard to which one would compare any policy choice?

CONCLUSION

Advance directives and living wills have been heralded as the answer to the awkward problem of how to empower patients so that they maintain control of their care even when incompetent. The jury is still out in terms of whether they are useful or not. Possibly the question ought to be posed: how ought we define and implement an optimal procedure to make care decisions on behalf of incompetent adults? It remains uncertain how adequately advance directives answer that need, particularly in comparison with possible alternatives. The debate about advance directives has helped to focus attention on the ethical, medical and legal issues in the treatment of incompetent patients. Perhaps the next step is for a consideration of what quality of life for incompetent patients is worth protecting.

Nine

What the Public Say

1994 saw the deaths of two world figures in quick succession: Richard Nixon and Jacqueline Onassis. The manner of their deaths, like so much of their lives, were significant. Both deaths reflected a quiet but pervasive revolution in the social attitude to dying: a willingness to say no to 'futile care' that merely postpones the inevitable. Onassis decided to halt antibiotic treatment for pneumonia and leave the hospital after her doctors told her they could do nothing more to treat her advanced lymphonia, an immune-cell cancer. Nixon decided in advance against being hooked up to an artificial breathing machine, an order his doctors honoured after the former president suffered a stroke, even though respirator treatment might have prolonged his life. One ethicist observed: 'These two deaths show the possibilities of thinking about death as the end of a journey rather than what happens when you drive the medical car full speed off the edge of a cliff.'

Onassis and Nixon, in the manner of their dying, expressed a widespread yearning for a less medically intrusive demise that is finding everyday expression in

US hospitals. A landmark $US28 million study presented in May 1994 at the American Geriatric Society meeting in Los Angeles, found that most dying patients or their families now decide against resuscitation efforts in the event of cardiac arrest. In a finding with major implications for US health-care reform, the study contradicts the widespread belief that the nation wastes billions of dollars on futile care for terminally ill patients. Only 'modest' savings are possible by forgoing care that merely prolonged dying, the study found. Even for the small group of critically ill patients with the highest expectation of death, the study found, only $US1 of every $US8 in medical-care costs could be saved by a hard-and-fast policy that ruled out life-prolonging care. Moreover, these savings would come largely by withholding care from the relatively young critically ill patients, a policy, the study's authors noted, which would be unpalatable both to the public and to medical caregivers. This is true in large part, the authors and others say, because American physicians, patients and families are already withholding or stopping treatment when it becomes obvious that further care is pointless.

In the new study, for example, doctors attempted to resuscitate only 14 per cent of the 1150 critically ill patients who died during the project. The study enrolled 4301 patients with nine life-threatening diagnoses – such as coma, heart failure and advanced lung cancer – who survived at least 48 hours after admission to the hospital. In the 1970s and early 1980s, doctors would have attempted to resuscitate the vast majority of such critically patients if they suffered cardiac arrest, said Dr Joanne Lynn of Dartmouth Medical School, the project's leader.

While attitudes to dying appear to be changing, what of attitudes to euthanasia? One of the problems in attempting to answer the question is that we are very short on information about attitudes to euthanasia on the part of health-care professionals and the public at large.

THE VIEW FROM DOWN UNDER

In August 1991 a survey was conducted concerning the management of death, dying and euthanasia and focused on the findings concerning the attitudes and practices of doctors in South Australia. Mail-back, self-administered questionnaires were posted to a ten per cent sample of 494 medical practitioners randomly selected from the list published by the Medical Board of South Australia. A total response rate of 68 per cent was obtained, 60 per cent of which (298) were usable returns. The survey found that 47 per cent had received requests from patients to hasten their deaths. 19 per cent had taken active steps which had brought about the death of a patient. Sixty-eight per cent thought that guidelines for withholding and withdrawal of treatment should be established. 45 per cent were in favour of the legislation of active euthanasia under certain circumstances.

In 1985 a Gallup poll in the United States asked a sample of the general public whether they believed that the law should make possible the withholding of life-sustaining medical treatment if that was what a patient wanted. Those 65 and older were significantly less in favour of such a law than younger people. Sixty-eight per cent of those 65 and older and favoured it, 20 per cent were opposed and 12 per cent had no opinion. The national average for all age groups was 81 per cent in favour, 13 per cent opposed and 6 per cent with no opinion.

'DEATH WITH DIGNITY'

One test of popular opinion which attracted a lot of attention in 1991 was 'Washington state measure 119' which would have made it legal deliberately to end the life of a terminal patient. It was the second attempt through the mechanism of a referendum to legislate making some form of euthanasia legal in the United States. The first had been defeated in California two years previously.

From the outset Washington's, 'death with dignity' campaign had the look of a winner. Everything seemed to be falling into place – to an extent which took even its most ardent supporters by surprise. Right up to the last moment it seemed that the Initiative would be passed – creating history by making Washington the first place in the world to legalise voluntary euthanasia for the terminally ill.

The first task of the lobby group supporting the measure was to gather the 150,001 signatures necessary to place the measure on the ballot. This they did with ease. The prime mover was the president of the Hemlock society of Washington state, who gathered 1,200 signatures in a single weekend with the assistance of just one volunteer. Money flooded in – from no less than 26,000 individual contributors.

Their opposition was an uncomfortable and badly organised umbrella group of a number of right-to-life groups, the Catholic Church, born-in-again Christian groups and – belatedly – the Washington State Medical Association. Members squabbled over details, had little money, no obvious campaign strategy and, in short, appeared to be fighting a losing battle. A symptom of their disarray was that less than two months before the election, their campaign office did not even have a listed telephone number.

Public opinion polls indicated the 'pro' side would win comfortably. Yet, as Charlie Haughey was wont to say: 'The only poll that matters is an election.' When the votes were tallied, the 'pro' side lost by a clear-cut margin, having secured just 46 per cent of 1.5 million votes cast. The reversal in their fortunes is the stuff of a Hollywood blockbuster.

In the course of the campaign it was claimed that Initiative 119 was the fruit of a plot of the international right-to-die movement – which had targeted Washington as the most likely place in the world to insert the thin end of the euthanasia wedge. This is a misrepresentation. In actual fact, members of the local Hemlock Society independently got the ball rolling, although they were obviously influenced by the wording of the Hemlock-sponsored referendum in California in 1988, the so-called Humane and Dignified Death Act. Nonetheless the Washington group could not have chosen a more suitable venue or timing.

Washington is one of only 22 states that have an initiative process, and since its population is only five million, it is an ideal stomping ground for would-be reformers. Moreover, by tradition Washington voters have a reputation as mavericks, with no qualms about crossing conventional lines. Personal autonomy is zealously defended. In addition, organised religions have a more tenuous foothold in the Pacific Northwest than in any other part of the country, for example according to one study only 19 per cent of Washingtonians consider themselves Catholic, significantly lower than the national average of 26.2 per cent

However, it was the timing of Initiative 119 that appeared to turn the tide firmly towards the pro-side. It came at a time when the general public were exasperated with the state's existing right-to-die law, i.e. the Natural Death Act (1979). While that law had been heralded as a great leap forward, the passage of time had caused it to be perceived as excessively restrictive. A popular perception that some new measure was necessary allowed the advocates behind I-119 to present aid-in-dying not as a stand-alone issue but as part of a package deal, one of several changes that constituted a substantial reform. In rewriting the existing law, they were able to incorporate features that local health-care professionals had attempted to get through the state legislature for three consecutive years without success.

Apart from adding a provision which would have legitimatised 'aid-in-dying' to competent, terminally ill adults, 119 would have broadened the state's definition of 'terminal condition' to include patients with up to six months to live and also those who were not actually about to die, but in irreversible comas or persistent vegetative states. It would also have explicitly listed nutrition and hydration as life sustaining procedures that could be refused in living wills. The anti side accused their opponents of wilful deception – attempting to slip in the euthanasia option under the pretext of more acceptable changes.

ON THE HUSTINGS

The campaign caught the imagination of the general public because it tested, for the first time, what would happen if this most difficult of moral dilemmas were put to the vote. Campaigners on both sides found themselves in virgin territory because of the difficulty of reducing complicated arguments to compelling sound bytes.

The campaign was a great spectator sport because it was debated with such ferocity and passion. Both groups campaigned in the certitude that they were taking a stand for the good of humankind, and each verbally attacked the other with undisguised hostility. Patients were interviewed for their thoughts literally from their deathbed, which made for gripping viewing and listening. The debate was conducted in the full glare of media publicity, with media commentators from virtually every corner of the globe in attendance. A *Who's Who* of philosophers, ethicists and leading physicians were given a platform to air their views and all the usual suspects (fanatics on both sides) were wheeled in. Four ingredients added to this explosive cocktail: a best-selling book, a damning suicide note, the wealth of the Catholic Church, and what one commentator called 'the wild excesses of an out-of-control physician'.

The euthanasia dimension was significantly underplayed during the signature drive and in the early days of the campaign. The petition the pro side distributed stated: *Death with Dignity and a Voluntary Choice for Terminally Ill Persons*. The word, 'euthanasia' was never used. A soaring dove was silhouetted in one section. Moreover, the wording of the actual legislation was sanitised: 'Shall adult patients who are in a medically terminal condition be permitted to request and receive from a physician aid-in-dying?' Eventually it became public knowledge that 'physician aid-in-dying' was code for active euthanasia.

The proponents of 119 attempted to sell the entire 119 package, spending a great deal of time and effort making arguments about non-controversial issues, e.g. living wills and tube feeding. The tactic was to get people to concentrate on the pain and frustration of the terminally ill, because the public would then be more likely to back all attempts to give control to the patient. With that in view they sought to achieve an educational programme particularly in relation to opinion setters. They organised hundreds of such educational forums. They stressed that aid-in-dying would be completely voluntary on the part of both doctor and patient, that in order to qualify a patient would have to be have to be conscious, competent, and request aid-in-dying in writing. Moreover, two doctors, one of them the attending doctor, would be required to certify that the patient had six months or less to live.

The No campaign tried to undermine these arguments one by one – claiming that there was no guarantee the law would be followed with respect to the safeguards mentioned above. In addition, there was a very real prospect, they claimed, of patients being killed against their will, either because of misguided doctors, because killing would be a cheap alternative to expensive terminal care, or because patients would be coerced by impatient or avaricious family members.

Initially the No campaign was hampered by a lack of finances, but as the election drew closer, money flowed into the 119 vote No campaign in ever increasing amounts from right-to-life groups and the Catholic Church, much of it from outside the state. The Catholic Church launched an all-out blitz, not only with financial backing but also with support from the altar and in the streets, by arranging a drive for new-voter registration, making absentee ballots, and urging donations. Archbishop Thomas Murphy made a national appeal which yielded $340,000.

The No side also took their campaign to television

with a series of controversial advertisements. The Yes side used the obvious ploy of having terminally ill cancer patients stare into the camera and argue for their right to choose 'a dignified death'. Their opponents were even more emotive, and appeared not unduly concerned if their ads strayed over the boundaries of the truth. A kindly hospice nurse said: 'Initiative 119 would let doctors kill my patients.' Another said: 'In Holland, the only place where doctors are permitted to put patients to death, thousands were killed or allowed to die last year alone – without being asked'. A third stated: 'An eye doctor could put you to death.' One of the most striking ads used an elderly farmer walking on his land, talking about his death and claiming: 'The problem with Initiative 119 is it gives some people too much authority to take someone else's life... It is more or less a right to kill.' While the word DEATH flashed on the screen, in white letters on a black background, he closed his comments with the words: 'There should be no law to take your life away from you.' These ads disgusted the Yes campaigners, because they saw them as total falsehood. Even more worrying was the fact they were powerless to counteract them. They were to discover just how easy it is to spread fear.

The medical profession was divided about the campaign – with equally vociferous and strident campaigners on both sides. The official policy-making organ of the state's doctors, Washington State Medical Association (WSMA), voted overwhelmingly to oppose 119 in consecutive annual meetings of delegates in September 1990 and 1991. The delegates were subsequently criticised for taking such a stance without having initially polled individual physicians. Accordingly, a sample poll was taken which produced a bewildering set of results. 75 per cent of doctors answered that they did not believe they should have the right to give a terminally ill patient a lethal injection. 60 per cent answered that physicians should not be permitted to prescribe a lethal dose of medication to be self-administered by the terminally ill patient. 75 per cent said they would not be willing to personally involved in aiding a patient's death. However, 543 of doctors polled expressed the view that the WSMA should support 119. This was almost identical to the figure, 562, who said that the WSMA should oppose it. The organisation's leadership refused to accept that these results indicated that half the doctors in Washington supported the concept of doctor aid-in-dying, claiming that physicians simply had not read the initiative. Two events were to create a sea-change in public opinion at large.

BEST SELLER

A feature of the 119 campaign was the prominence of the Hemlock Society and, in particular, its executive director, Derek Humphry. In October, Humphry's book *Final Exit*, effectively a suicide manual, became a runaway bestseller. Humphry became a seemingly ever-present face on television screens, promoting the book. Then when the hype was at its height Humphry's ex-wife, Ann Wickett, took her own life by taking an overdose of drugs. In her suicide note, she accused Humphry of psychological cruelty that drove her to death. She then went on deliver the knockout punch, claiming that Humphry had actually smothered his first wife Jean, rather than simply providing her with lethal drugs, as he claimed in his first book, *Jean's Way*. Not surprisingly, Humphry put up a vigorous defence, even to the extent of taking out a quarter-page ad in the *New York Times* to draw attention to his ex-wife's mental problems. Nonetheless, he came off badly from the affair and the Yes campaign suffered a severe body blow.

To compound the Yes side's woe, just eleven days before the election the controversial Dr Jack Kevorkian made a dramatic entrance into the campaign. The previous year this Michigan pathologist had created a storm with his 'suicide machine' which helped people to take their own lives. As the campaign entered its final countdown, Kevorkian assisted in the suicides of two women, neither of whom was terminally ill, in a Michigan cabin.

Up to that point, Washington polls had shown an unusually large number of 'undecided' on the 119 issue. In the wake of five days of blanket coverage of Kevorkian, the floating voters rowed in firmly behind the No campaign. On election night after the polls closed at eight p.m., the first tally showed that in one precinct of a total of 200 votes cast, 70 per cent were yeses. It was the only time the Yes side would have the ascendancy, and the result was a decisive victory for the No side.

Conclusion

Never before have the possibilities open to humankind been so great. Yet hand in hand with exciting developments in science and health care, a certain fear has taken root, a fear of what might be called the dehumanisation of medicine. A consequence of the increasing technology is that the traditional ethical question has been turned on its head. Historically, ethicists have asked the question: how can people be brought to do what they ought? Today increasingly ethicists are asking: when should people be restrained from doing all that they are capable of? Medical dilemmas are bewildering because doctors and families want to act in the best interests of patients, but are unsure about the scope and content of the obligation to care.

An adequate ethical framework in relation to the treatment of the terminally ill patients is not just a mere individualistic situation ethic – one which points to the uniqueness of each case, but one in which the norms inform the situation and, *vice versa*, the situation determines the norms. Such an ethic provides basic convictions, basic attitudes, motivations and norms. What is required is a standpoint, an orientation, a coordinating system, a compass.

A new attitude to treatment is a further consequence

of the respect due to every human being. It is not just a matter of treating illness, a disease, but of seeing the people who are ill, and of recognising that every form of care for human life is meaningful. In the past doctors have referred to the rule of double effect, built on the distinction between direct and indirect intentions and consequences of actions. Although this has been a prominent feature in the discussion of abortion, it is of little value in the care of terminally ill patients. We have to ask why and at what cost we allow different classes of patients, such as seriously defective newborns and comatose patients, to die.

In ethical discussion of the treatment of terminally ill patients, as in any other area of ethics, there must always be room for exceptions. For instance, in the course of the Falklands war a soldier was reported to have shot his trapped comrade in response to his comrade's anguished pleas that he was burning to death in a situation from which there was no possibility of saving him. Was that morally wrong? The duty to respect life may conflict with obligation to minimise suffering and to respect autonomy. It is a cliché, but a truth none the less, that hard cases make for bad law. Good ethics depend on good facts. It may therefore be desirable to have a rule of practice that prohibits direct killing and authorises allowing some patients to die in some circumstances, even if this rule fails to fit every exceptional case that might be encountered or imagined.

A French biologist once said: 'Humans have become much too powerful to be allowed to be playing with evil. Their power in excess condemns them to virtue.' If only it were so simple. As we have seen, language is critical in this entire debate. For example, in the case of the phrase 'mercy killing', there is something incongruous about saying that it is being kind to someone to say that they should cease to exist. Decisions about euthanasia involve considerations about the patient's best interests and personal choices, but they are also influenced by questions of paternalism and the allocation of scarce resources. Caring ought not be identified with curing, but with our willingness to be with others even though they are dying. Optimal care ought not to be equated with maximal treatment. Keeping a person alive at all costs is a form of biological idolatry.

The questions we have discussed are not just matters for esoteric discussion. Our society's willingness and ability to protect vulnerable life hang in the balance.

Selected Bibliography

Augenstein, Leroy, *Come, Let Us Play God*, New York: Harper & Row, 1969.

Beauchamp, Tom L., *Philosophical Ethics*, New York: McGraw-Hill, 1982. Baird, R. and Rosenbaum, S. (eds), *Euthanasia: The Moral Issues*, New York: Prometheus Books, 1989.

Brody, B., *Suicide and Euthanasia*, London: Kluewer Academic Publishers, 1989.

Callahan, Daniel, 'Bioethics as a Discipline', *Hastings Center Studies*, 1 (1973), 66-73.

————, "The Ethics Backlash", *Hastings Center Report*, 5 (August 1975), 18.

Campbell, A. V., *Moral Dilemmas in Medicine*, Baltimore: The Williams & Wilkins Company, 1975.

Conwell, Y. et al., 'Completed Suicide at Age 50 and Over', *Journal of the American Geriatrics Society* 1990; 38(6) June: 640-644.

Costello, Declan, 'The Terminally Ill: The Law's Concerns', *Doctrine and Life* Vol 38, Feb 1988, pp 69-78.

Curran, Charles E., *Politics, Medicine and Christian Ethics*, Philadelphia: Fortress Press, 1973.

Fletcher, Joseph, *Morals and Medicine*, Boston: Beacon Press, 1954.

Frankena, William K., *Ethics*, Englewood Cliffs, N.J.: Prentice-Hall, 1973.

Gillon, Raanan, 'Medicine, Profession and Society', *Journal of Medical Ethics*, 11 (1985), 59-61.

————, 'More on Professional Ethics', *Journal of Medical Ethics*, 12 (1986), 62.

Gustafson, J. M., *Theology and Christian Ethics*, Philadelphia: United Church Press, 1974.

Hare, R. M., *The Language of Morals*, Oxford: Oxford University Press, 1962.

Hauerwas, Stanley, *Suffering Presence*, Notre Dame Press, 1986.

Heyer, Robert, *Medical and Legal Intersections*, New Haven: Paulist Press, 1977.

Illich, Ivan, *Medical Nemesis*, New York: Pantheon Books, 1976.

Kelly, Gerald, *Medico-Moral Problems*, St Louis Catholic Hospital Association, 1958.

Leach, Gerald, *The Biocrats*, New York: Penguin Books, 1972.

McCormick, Richard, *Ambiguity in Moral Choice*, Milwaukee: Marquette University Press, 1973.

————, *The Critical Calling*, Milwaukee: Marquette University Press, 1989.

MacIntyre, Alasdair, *Whose Justice? Which Rationality?* London: Duckworth, 1988.

Mill, John Stuart, *On Liberty*, London: J.W. Parker, 1859.

Ramsey, Paul, *Ethics at the Edge of Life*, New Haven: Yale University Press, 1978.

————, *The Patient as Person*, New Haven: Yale University Press, 1970.

Rawls, John, *A Theory of Justice*, Cambridge, Mass.: Harvard University Press, 1971.

Reidy, Maurice, *Foundations for a Medical Ethic*, Dublin: Veritas, 1977.

Sigerist, Henry E., *A History Of Medicine*, New York: Oxford University Press, 1972.

Shaw, A., 'Defining the Quality of Life' *Hastings Center Report*, October 1977, p.11

Stout, Jeffrey, *Ethics after Babel: The Languages of Morals and their Discontents*, Edinburgh, James Clark, 1990.

Talbot, C.H., *Medicine in England*, London: Oldbourne Book Company, 1967.

van der Mass, P. *et al.*, "Euthanasia and Other Medical Decisions concerning the End of life", *The Lancet*, 14 September 1991